Welfare

Other Books of Related Interest:

Opposing Viewpoints Series

Poverty

Current Controversies Series

Illegal Immigration

"Congress shall make
no law . . . abridging
the freedom of speech,
or of the press."

First Amendment to the U.S. Constitution

The basic foundation of our democracy is the First Amendment guarantee of freedom of expression. The *Opposing Viewpoints* Series is dedicated to the concept of this basic freedom and the idea that it is more important to practice it than to enshrine it.

OPPOSING VIEWPOINTS® SERIES

Welfare

David M. Haugen and Andrea B. DeMott, Book Editors

GREENHAVEN PRESS
A part of Gale, Cengage Learning

GALE
CENGAGE Learning

Detroit • New York • San Francisco • New Haven, Conn • Waterville, Maine • London

GALE
CENGAGE Learning

Christine Nasso, *Publisher*
Elizabeth Des Chenes, *Managing Editor*

© 2008 Greenhaven Press, a part of Gale, Cengage Learning

Gale and Greenhaven Press are registered trademarks used herein under license.

For more information, contact:
Greenhaven Press
27500 Drake Rd.
Farmington Hills, MI 48331-3535
Or you can visit our Internet site at gale.cengage.com

For product information and technology assistance, contact us at

Gale Customer Support, 1-800-877-4253
For permission to use material from this text or product, submit all requests online at www.cengage.com/permissions

Further permissions questions can be emailed to permissionrequest@cengage.com

Articles in Greenhaven Press anthologies are often edited for length to meet page requirements. In addition, original titles of these works are changed to clearly present the main thesis and to explicitly indicate the author's opinion. Every effort is made to ensure that Greenhaven Press accurately reflects the original intent of the authors. Every effort has been made to trace the owners of copyrighted material.

Cover photograph © Daniel Allan/Taxi/Getty Images.

LIBRARY OF CONGRESS CATALOGING-IN-PUBLICATION DATA

Welfare / David M. Haugen and Andrea B. DeMott, book editors.
    p. cm. -- (Opposing viewpoints)
    Includes bibliographical references and index.
    ISBN 978-0-7377-4016-5 (hardcover)
    ISBN 978-0-7377-4017-2 (pbk.)
    1. Public welfare--United States. 2. Welfare recipients--United States. 3. Aid to families with dependent children programs--United States. I. Haugen, David M., 1969- II. DeMott, Andrea B.
    HV91.W4662 2008
    362.5'5680973--dc22
                                                                    2008010059

Contents

Chapter 3: How Can the Welfare System Discourage Dependence?

Chapter 4: What Are Some Alternatives to the Current Welfare System?

Why Consider Opposing Viewpoints?

> "The only way in which a human being can make some approach to knowing the whole of a subject is by hearing what can be said about it by persons of every variety of opinion and studying all modes in which it can be looked at by every character of mind. No wise man ever acquired his wisdom in any mode but this."
>
> *John Stuart Mill*

In our media-intensive culture it is not difficult to find differing opinions. Thousands of newspapers and magazines and dozens of radio and television talk shows resound with differing points of view. The difficulty lies in deciding which opinion to agree with and which "experts" seem the most credible. The more inundated we become with differing opinions and claims, the more essential it is to hone critical reading and thinking skills to evaluate these ideas. *Opposing Viewpoints* books address this problem directly by presenting stimulating debates that can be used to enhance and teach these skills. The varied opinions contained in each book examine many different aspects of a single issue. While examining these conveniently edited opposing views, readers can develop critical thinking skills such as the ability to compare and contrast authors' credibility, facts, argumentation styles, use of persuasive techniques, and other stylistic tools. In short, the *Opposing Viewpoints* Series is an ideal way to attain the higher-level thinking and reading skills so essential in a culture of diverse and contradictory opinions.

In addition to providing a tool for critical thinking, *Opposing Viewpoints* books challenge readers to question their own strongly held opinions and assumptions. Most people form their opinions on the basis of upbringing, peer pressure, and personal, cultural, or professional bias. By reading carefully balanced opposing views, readers must directly confront new ideas as well as the opinions of those with whom they disagree. This is not to simplistically argue that everyone who reads opposing views will—or should—change his or her opinion. Instead, the series enhances readers' understanding of their own views by encouraging confrontation with opposing ideas. Careful examination of others' views can lead to the readers' understanding of the logical inconsistencies in their own opinions, perspective on why they hold an opinion, and the consideration of the possibility that their opinion requires further evaluation.

Evaluating Other Opinions

To ensure that this type of examination occurs, *Opposing Viewpoints* books present all types of opinions. Prominent spokespeople on different sides of each issue as well as well-known professionals from many disciplines challenge the reader. An additional goal of the series is to provide a forum for other, less known, or even unpopular viewpoints. The opinion of an ordinary person who has had to make the decision to cut off life support from a terminally ill relative, for example, may be just as valuable and provide just as much insight as a medical ethicist's professional opinion. The editors have two additional purposes in including these less known views. One, the editors encourage readers to respect others' opinions—even when not enhanced by professional credibility. It is only by reading or listening to and objectively evaluating others' ideas that one can determine whether they are worthy of consideration. Two, the inclusion of such viewpoints encourages the important critical thinking skill of objectively evaluating an author's credentials and bias. This evaluation will illuminate an author's reasons for taking a particular stance on an issue and will aid in readers' evaluation of the author's ideas.

It is our hope that these books will give readers a deeper understanding of the issues debated and an appreciation of the complexity of even seemingly simple issues when good and honest people disagree. This awareness is particularly important in a democratic society such as ours in which people enter into public debate to determine the common good. Those with whom one disagrees should not be regarded as enemies but rather as people whose views deserve careful examination and may shed light on one's own.

Thomas Jefferson once said that "difference of opinion leads to inquiry, and inquiry to truth." Jefferson, a broadly educated man, argued that "if a nation expects to be ignorant and free . . . it expects what never was and never will be." As individuals and as a nation, it is imperative that we consider the opinions of others and examine them with skill and discernment. The *Opposing Viewpoints* Series is intended to help readers achieve this goal.

David L. Bender and Bruno Leone,
Founders

Introduction

> "If it seems shocking to speak about poverty in moral terms, to regard someone's squalor as the result of his lack of character and values—then that is because the moral assumptions behind the welfare state have been so widely and uncritically accepted. In the welfare statist's world, no one is responsible for his own life. People's lives are shaped by social forces, not by their own choices. Because "society" makes people poor, in this view, "society" owes them handouts. This unquestioned assumption is the welfare debate we're not having."
>
> —Robert W. Tracinski,
> editor and publisher of the
> Intellectual Activist, a pro-reason,
> pro-individualist magazine.

The modern American welfare state is a product of New Deal legislation that was designed to blunt the effects of the Great Depression of the 1930s. As part of the Social Security Act of 1935, the federal government set up a program called Aid to Dependent Children (ADC) to provide block grants to states to supplement state funds used primarily to support the children of single mothers. Originally the law did not clarify which children were eligible, but over the first thirty years of service, ADC was revised to designate that its cash assistance could only be distributed to "suitable" families. In effect, the stigma of illegitimacy and social divisions based on race kept many families from receiving assistance. In addition, caseworkers routinely visited ADC recipients to make sure suitable environments for childrearing were maintained. Thus, welfare began not as an egalitarian program to assist the nation's poor but as one guided by notions of social decency and prejudice.

Decades later, the government revised ADC, allowing the program to move beyond its original aim of assisting "dependent children." In 1963 the program was renamed Aid to Families with Dependent Children (AFDC) to note that assistance was being given to single-parent families as well as two-parent families in which the father was unemployed. Later in the decade, the federal statutes even permitted any other "essential person" in a family with dependent children to claim welfare benefits. States, however, were free to interpret these allowances as they saw fit, and not all handed out welfare so liberally. Yet eventually the moral standards of resistant states came under fire. For instance, in the 1968 U.S. Supreme Court case *King v. Smith*, the Court struck down a welfare clause in Alabama that sanctioned the denial of benefits to single mothers who had even casual relationships with men.

As illegitimacy and licentious behaviors became slowly divorced from welfare restrictions, they remained part of the governmental and popular conceptions of welfare clientele. In addition, these stigmas were increasingly tied to the African American community in the 1960s. As lecturer and writer Andrew Bernstein states, "Because a disproportionate number of black Americans were poor in the late 1960s, and because the Civil Rights Movement of that era was an attempt to redress a century of racial injustices, the government's war on poverty coalesced into a campaign heavily (though not exclusively) directed toward blacks." Bernstein goes on to note that a rise in illegitimate births among blacks in the mid-1960s prompted assistant secretary of labor Daniel Patrick Moynihan to see the "disintegration of the family as the single greatest problem confronting black Americans." While Bernstein's assessment of Moynihan's views is debatable, Moynihan did consider illegitimacy as a contributing factor in the decline of strong male leadership in the African American community. Moynihan contended that finding employment for black men would be a better solution for the nation than fostering a continual state of welfare dependence.

Noting the rise in welfare disbursements and the eroding eligibility requirements for enrolling in these programs (which during President Lyndon Johnson's administration expanded to include Medicaid and food stamps), critics suggested that many welfare recipients were abusing the system. In response, the federal government began to compel states to deny benefits to recipients who were unemployed without good reason. In 1962, Congress authorized the funding of Community Work and Training programs (CWTs) to decrease the number of supposed hangers-on by paying "trainees" as they built job skills. This program was supplemented in 1968 by the Work Incentives program (WIN) that required unemployed fathers to register for job training. In 1971 the WIN registration requirements were extended to all adult welfare recipients except mothers of very young children.

By the 1980s, the benefits of the welfare-to-work programs were in doubt. African American earnings stagnated in the decade, and several nationwide reports concluded that more than half of welfare recipients remained on the rolls for eight years or longer. Then, two influential books weighed in on the dangers of prolonging the welfare state. In 1984 conservative scholar Charles Murray published *Losing Ground*, in which he maintained that welfare payments encouraged single-motherhood and sanctioned promiscuity because of the income that could be garnered by unwed mothers with multiple children. Murray's work was followed in 1986 by Lawrence Mead's *Beyond Entitlement*. Mead, a professor of political science, asserted that government mandated but locally controlled welfare-to-work programs were the solution to breaking the unending cycle of welfare. The federal government had already gotten part of Mead's message. In 1981, Congress gave states the power to create their own welfare-to-work programs in an effort to broaden if not mandate welfare-to-work opportunities.

Enforcing work requirements in the 1980s also became popular because of President Ronald Reagan's vilification of supposed welfare cheats. In making his own bid to reform welfare, Reagan often referred to a black "welfare queen" in Chicago who, as he claimed, scammed the welfare system by applying for benefits under several aliases and ended up touring the city in a Cadillac while collecting welfare checks. Reagan's critics pointed out that the president never gave evidence that such an egregious con-woman existed, but his perpetual use of the image made many believe that the poor—especially the African American poor—were living off the proceeds of white taxpayers. His solution was to limit dependence and bring back the supposedly lost integrity of work. Or as progressive journalist Gary Delgado writes in a 2000 issue of *Colorlines*, Reagan and his cronies "managed to convince many people that, for poor women and children, depending on one source of money (welfare) was pathological, while depending on benefit-less, low-wage labor was ennobling."

All of these sinister images of welfare recipients and their lifestyles informed political discussions on Capitol Hill and in the White House through the administration of President Bill Clinton. Michael Tanner, the director of health and welfare studies at the libertarian Cato Institute, clarified what he and others saw as the evils of welfare in testimony before the Senate Finance Committee in March 1995. He argued that the problems of welfare have little to do with excessive government spending: "The real welfare crisis lies in what the system is doing to our society. . . . There is strong evidence that links the availability of welfare with the increase in out-of-wedlock births," Tanner stated, "[and] by removing the economic consequences of a[n] out-of-wedlock birth, welfare has removed a major incentive to avoid such pregnancies." Tanner went on to draw a link between welfare and crime, stating, "Welfare contributes to crime by destroying the family structure and breaking down the bonds of community. Moreover, it contributes to the social marginalization of young black men by making them irrelevant to the family." He furthered the argument by warning that "there is strong evidence that the absence of a father [in single-parent families] increases the probability that a child will use drugs and engage in criminal activity."

Tanner informed Congress that the solution to these problems was the complete dismantling of the welfare system, and some in the Republican majorities that held Capitol Hill were receptive to the notion. Most lawmakers, however, eventually fell in behind President Bill Clinton's proposal to increase work requirements for those receiving benefits. Clinton had just campaigned for the White House on a pledge to "end welfare as we know it," and the Republican Congress was eager to hold him to that promise. On August 22, 1996, the president signed a bipartisan bill that was more restrictive than his original proposal. The Personal Responsibility and Work Opportunity Reconciliation Act (PRWORA) enforced welfare-to-work policies by denying benefits to able adult recipients who were not actively seeking employment. The law also set a sixty-month cap on the length of time a recipient could claim benefits. AFDC was terminated, and benefits were also strictly handed out by the states, which received block grants—known as Temporary Assistance to Needy Families (TANF)—from the federal government to implement their own welfare programs. The states were also rewarded financially for moving claimants off the welfare rolls as quickly as possible.

In addition to the work mandates, the new legislation contained provisions to insist on personal responsibility among welfare recipients. Child support measures made it harder for noncustodial parents to evade payments. A cap on family benefits held cash assistance steady regardless of further out-of-wedlock births. New guidelines required that teen parents claiming benefits had to be in the custody of a parent or guardian and attending school. And teen pregnancy prevention programs were established to promote abstinence education. In his assessment of the PRWORA, Brookings Institution scholar Ron Haskins attests, "Taken together, these provisions were by far the most forceful attack the federal government had ever mounted against illegitimacy."

In 2006, the PRWORA was scheduled for reauthorization. The law had reduced welfare rolls across the nation by 50 percent, and large numbers of single mothers had joined the workforce seemingly without ill effects. President George W. Bush hoped to capitalize on the success to promote his own welfare reform agenda in the new millennium. While maintaining a strong welfare-to-work ethic, the president's plan emphasized the role of nongovernmental organizations in aiding the needy. A prominent aspect of the plan was helping faith-based organizations find federal money that could be used to provide welfare services at the community level. Another noteworthy element was the Healthy Marriage Initiative. Inaugurated by President Bush in 2002, this program began researching how the government could best support the maintenance of two-parent families and thus reduce the problems of out-of-wedlock births and absentee fathers. In 2005, Congress approved $150 million in funding to be awarded to national, state, or local demonstration projects focusing on marriage education, marriage skills training, public advertising campaigns, high school education on the value of marriage, and marriage mentoring programs. Explaining the value of the program, Wade F. Horn, the assistant secretary for children and families at the U.S. Department of Health and Human Services, asserts, "The aim . . . of the president's Healthy Marriage Initiative is to give low-income couples greater access to marriage-education services and thereby improve their chances of forming healthy, stable marriages."

Sharon Lerner, a senior fellow at the Center for New York City Affairs at New School University, is one critic of the moralistic overtones of the president's Healthy Marriage Initiative. She insists that the plan's logic is faulty. Instead of promoting marriage to end poverty, the administration, in Lerner's view, should be tackling poverty and other social ills that hinder many poor people from getting married. Unlike supporters of the Healthy Marriage Initiative, Lerner sees social ills such as poverty and domestic violence as obstacles to overcoming welfare dependence. And like several other critics of modern welfare reform, Lerner fears that government programs are still trying to legislate personal behavior and penalizing those families who are still deemed unsuitable.

Lerner's viewpoint is one of many anthologized in *Opposing Viewpoints: Welfare*. Hers is part of the debate that is waged in the chapter entitled How Do Welfare Policies Affect Families? The remaining chapters of the anthology organize further debate around the questions: Is Welfare Reform Working? How Can the Welfare System Discourage Dependence? and What Are Some Alternatives to the Current Welfare System? In all these chapters, post-welfare-reform programs are assessed not only for their impact on poverty but also for their implicit or explicit judgments on the moral well-being of America. The notion of the welfare state was born out of a moral imperative—the sense of duty to help the less fortunate. But since its inception, that duty—or perhaps the extent of that duty—has been questioned. As this anthology demonstrates, the contemporary welfare debate is still driven not only by concerns about spending but also by conflicting notions of decency and personal responsibility.

CHAPTER 1

Is Welfare Reform Working?

Chapter Preface

The effects of the 1996 Personal Responsibility and Work Opportunity Reconciliation Act that summarily destroyed the welfare state, which had existed since the New Deal of the 1930s, have been dramatic. With welfare-to-work strategies enforced, the number of Americans on government welfare rolls dropped by half within four years of the law's enactment. The flood of former welfare recipients into the workforce brought concern that the poverty rate would increase, and though it indeed did rise during the recession at the beginning of the twenty-first century, the rate has declined between 2006 and 2007 as the economy recovers. Olivia Golden, a former assistant secretary for children and families in the U.S. Department of Health and Human Services, sees the trend toward wider employment among welfare recipients as good news: "It means that low-income families now look much more like other American families: In most, parents are working many hours while also raising children."

Golden and others, however, are quick to point out that the cuts in the poverty rolls do not indicate that former welfare clients were suddenly pushed far up the economic ladder by acquiring jobs. "Nationally, the economic picture for families who left welfare is mixed," Golden states. "Though many are connected to the labor market, others are not. Wages are low although comparable to those of low-skill workers who have not been on welfare. And the overall picture for these families, as for other needy families, got worse as the economy weakened in the early years of this decade." Nicole Colson, writing in the *Socialist Worker*, adds, "The truth is that many of the former welfare recipients who are considered 'success stories' have simply moved into the ranks of the working poor, trapped in low-wage jobs, usually with no benefits."

Proponents of welfare reform see the rise in the working poor more optimistically. In 2002 the Urban Institute reported that single mothers who were previously on the dole were earning around $8 an hour, which is more than $2 above minimum wage. Kay S. Hymowitz reported in a 2006 article for the *City Journal* that the wages plus tax credits were giving single mothers more income than they received from welfare. She also maintains that these working moms did not view their new jobs as dead-end positions. "Studies consistently found that ex-recipients who went on to become waitresses, grill cooks, and security guards took pride in being salary-women," Hymowitz states.

The authors in the following chapter debate the pros and cons of welfare reform and assess whether welfare-to-work policies achieved their intended goals more than a decade after the original legislation went into effect.

> *"Welfare reform has been a triumph for the federal government and the states."*

Welfare Reform Is Working

Ron Haskins

Ron Haskins is a senior fellow of economic studies and codirector of the Center on Children and Families at the Brookings Institution, a nonprofit public policy research organization. In the following viewpoint, Haskins states that government statistics and independent research have shown that welfare reform implemented in 1996 is working. He asserts that making employment a requisite for most welfare recipients and enacting federal policies designed to help low-income families have discouraged those on welfare to rely solely on government handouts. This has meant a drop in welfare cases and a rise in America's workforce, Haskins concludes.

As you read, consider the following questions:

1. By what percentage have welfare caseloads declined between 1994 and 2004, according to Haskins?
2. As the author reports, what percentage of adults leaving welfare hold at least one job?
3. What are the two additional factors that Haskins says contributed to favorable welfare-to-work outcomes?

It has been 10 years since the welfare reform law was signed by President [Bill] Clinton [in 1996] amid predictions of disaster from the left. Information reported by states, by the U.S. Census Bureau, and by researchers yields a coherent picture of the broad effects of the 1996 reforms.

Observational research conducted by Irene Lurie and her colleagues at the State University of New York shows that welfare case workers now consistently implement state policies designed to discourage families from relying on welfare by mandating employment-related activities and then by ensuring that clients participate in these activities. These changes constitute a revolution in social policy.

An Unprecedented Caseload Decline

What has been the effect of these major changes? Welfare caseloads began declining in the spring of 1994 and picked up steam after the federal legislation was enacted in 1996. Between 1994 and 2004, the caseload declined about 60 percent, a decline that is without precedent. The percentage of U.S. children on welfare is now lower than it has been since at least 1970.

But are the mothers who leave (or avoid) welfare able to find work? More than 40 studies conducted by states since 1996 show that about 60 percent of the adults leaving welfare are employed at any given moment and that, over a period of several months, about 80 percent hold at least one job. Even more impressive, national data from the Census Bureau show that between 1993 and 2000, the percentage of low-income, single mothers with a job grew from 58 percent to nearly 75 percent, an increase of almost 30 percent. Moreover, employment among never-married mothers, the most disadvantaged and least-educated subgroup of single mothers, grew from 44 percent to 66 percent, an increase of 50 percent, over the same period. Again, these sweeping changes are unprecedented.

Welfare Morphs into Work-Support Program

As caseloads declined, the states moved the federal money they would have spent on welfare benefits into work support—transportation, child care, and the like. In fact, under the states' management, welfare has morphed into an unprecedentedly generous work-support program. The real proof that the states were not the scoundrels that opponents had warned they would be came as Congress debated reauthorization after TANF [Temporary Assistance for Needy Families] expired in 2002. Reformers argued for even stricter federally mandated work requirements, while those who once warned that the states would engage in a race to the bottom demanded more state control.

This, then, is where we find ourselves today, ten years after reform: a record number of poor single mothers off the dole and the majority of them gainfully employed; less poverty among single mothers, especially black single mothers, as well as their kids; children adjusting well enough; and state governments taking care of their own.

Kay S. Hymowitz, City Journal, *spring 2006.*

Earnings Are Up

What about income? Census Bureau data show that in 1993, earnings accounted for about 30 percent of the income of low-income mother-headed families while welfare payments accounted for nearly 55 percent. By 2000, this pattern had reversed: earnings had leaped by an astounding 136 percent to constitute almost 57 percent of income while welfare income had plummeted by nearly half to constitute only about 23 percent of income. Equally important, with earnings leading the way, the total income of these low-income families increased by more than 25 percent over the period (in constant dollars).

Not surprisingly, between 1994 and 2000, child poverty fell every year and reached levels not seen since 1978. In addition, by 2000, the poverty rate of black children was the lowest it had ever been.

Critics point out that unemployment by single mothers has risen since the mild recession of 2001 and that child poverty has now increased for four consecutive years. Although unemployment has increased, there were 1.3 million more never-married mothers employed in 2002 than in 1993 before the economic expansion and the exodus from welfare reform. Moreover, even after four years of increases, the child poverty rate in 2004 was still 20 percent lower than in 1993.

Contributing Factors

Although welfare reform is a major cause of these felicitous outcomes, at least two additional factors are important. First, the economy of the 1990s was exceptionally strong and produced a net increase of 16 million jobs. Second, in the decade leading up to the welfare reform law and in the welfare reform law itself, Congress enacted a series of expansions in social programs—including child care, the child tax credit, Medicaid, the standard deduction and the personal exemption in the tax code, and the Earned Income Tax Credit—that were designed to help low-income families that work.

Clearly, federal social policy requiring work backed by sanctions and time limits while granting states the flexibility to design their own work programs produced better results than the previous policy of providing welfare benefits while expecting little in return. It is better to cajole mothers to take low-wage jobs and supplement their income rather than to allow them to languish on welfare. Above all, experience with welfare reform since 1996 shows conclusively that most low-income families are capable of finding and holding jobs while, with government support, increasing the financial well-being of their children. Welfare reform has been a triumph for the federal government and the states—and even more for single mothers.

> *"Although former [welfare] recipients are working more than ever before, their poverty has not significantly diminished, and their deprivation has in many instances increased."*

Welfare Reform Is Not Working

Cecilio Morales

Cecilio Morales argues in the following viewpoint that current "welfare-to-work" policies are not helping the poor. He claims that welfare reform was designed to help the needy secure benefits while gaining educational and work experience. In Morales's view, the government has reneged on that promise and is compelling welfare recipients to work more hours to earn their benefits, thus sacrificing time needed to attend school and maintain their families. Morales asserts that by pushing recipients to work more, the government is consigning the poor to low-paying, dead-end jobs that typically do not provide health insurance and are inadequate to meet the income needs of a family. Cecilio Morales is a journalist and the editor and publisher of two periodicals, Employment & Training Reporter *and* Welfare to Work.

As you read, consider the following questions:

1. As Morales reports, how many hours per week were welfare recipients expected to work under the Personal Responsibility and Work Opportunity Reconciliation Act?
2. What are "work supports," according to the author?
3. What did the Parents as Scholars program in Maine allow TANF recipients to do, according to Morales?

Hours after the 109th Congress convened in early January [2005], Republican majority leaders delivered this startling notice: they intend to transform public aid to the poor into a compulsory work program that offers little opportunity for recipients to lift themselves from poverty.

This transformation was the centerpiece of the blueprint President [George W.] Bush first unveiled on Feb. 26, 2002. Recipients of Temporary Assistance for Needy Families (TANF), the president said, should be compelled to work 40 hours a week. He did not point out that the proposal would eliminate the program's educational and support features, which have enabled at least some poor women with children to embark on self-sustaining careers instead of working at dead-end jobs that hold them in poverty.

For three years, only the qualms of moderate Senate Republicans and their Democratic colleagues managed to delay reauthorization of the program in the form Bush proposed. These doubters proposed instead to bolster efforts that would enable TANF recipients to earn employer-recognized educational credentials, address drug abuse and alcoholism problems, protect themselves from domestic abuse and provide care for their children as they embark on employment.

This difference of opinion goes to the heart of the dispute surrounding reauthorization of TANF, and indeed of all welfare reform dating back to policy compromises in the late

1980's. At that time, conservatives agreed to drop from their agenda the elimination of most forms of public aid, if liberals would agree to some form of required work.

The Welfare-to-Work Concept

President [Ronald] Reagan called it workfare. He tended to view the poor as indolent individuals with criminal leanings, as was indicated famously in his untrue story of the Chicago "welfare queen" who supposedly defrauded the public aid system using 80 aliases. Reagan argued that the poor should be compelled to earn their assistance money. To critics the idea was like a step backward to the Victorian workhouses, in which indigents, including children, were compelled to work and beaten at the slightest pretext. Reagan's critics, however, viewed the elimination of poverty, not of aid, as the proper goal.

Compromise brought about efforts designed to lead aid recipients to career objectives and, ultimately, unsubsidized employment. Officials at the Employment and Training Choices program in Massachusetts in the mid-1980's displayed an almost missionary zeal to transform lives socioeconomically when they begged me not to call their venture workfare in my reporting. I coined the phrase "welfare-to-work program," which later became the generally accepted term.

The concept inspired the 1988 experimental Job Opportunities and Basic Skills program, as well as its 20-hour rule, which required that for 20 hours every week, recipients would have to engage in work or related activities, which included training, unless their children were under 6. This requirement was included in the Personal Responsibility and Work Opportunity Reconciliation Act of 1996, which is still the current welfare law. In order to receive aid, which is limited to a lifetime maximum of five years, recipients would have to earn it by performing a required activity, preferably work.

Challenges of Low-Wage Work

For low-wage workers, many of the benefits available to higher earners are out of reach. Consider paid time off. More than half of poor workers, working welfare recipients and workers who recently left welfare are unable to take paid leave from their jobs because it's not offered, according to research by the Urban Institute.

While lower interest rates have made homeownership more affordable for many, runaway prices have put homes out of reach for the working poor. In the past 12 years, home prices have risen 30% faster than wages and salaries for low-to-moderate-income families, according to an April [2004] report by the Milken Institute.

While the economy has created nearly a million jobs since March [2004], the pace of job creation has previously been slow—taking a toll on lower-wage workers who often lack college degrees.

Stephanie Armour,
USA Today, June 9, 2004.

Building Career Opportunities

Yet for someone without a work history or suitable background, this is easier said than done. Every study available points to recipients' deficiencies in education and a wide range of behavioral problems that constitute barriers to employment. Moreover, the transition to work usually requires undergirding services known as work supports, which range from obtaining appropriate work clothes and transportation to having a subsidized child and health care. Even after getting a job, most TANF mothers need help when a child gets sick or the car breaks down. When such events occur, these women risk losing their foothold on the first rung of career ladders, since most supervisors of entry-level jobs do not tolerate unexpected absences.

The [Bill] Clinton administration interpreted the welfare reform act's requirements as an invitation to innovate, and a broad range of novel solutions ensued. In Maine, for instance, the Parents as Scholars program has allowed TANF recipients to live on campus with their children while earning nursing or technology-related degrees. In addition, children learn the value of education and work as they watch their mothers prepare to succeed. A thrift shop in Maryland turned into a retail work training center, but it also became the place where TANF women acquired their first workplace outfits. Goodwill Industries of Southern California began the Welfare-to-Work Job Readiness Program, offering comprehensive transition services to TANF recipients. The key to this program was its job coaches, who followed clients through training and for 90 days after they found their first jobs.

Still, these and many similar efforts have failed to fill yawning gaps. According to a federal estimate, for example, 14.7 million children in low-income families are eligible to receive subsidies for child care, but only 1.5 million actually receive them. Similarly, up to 64.9 percent of women receiving some kind of public benefit reported being abused in various ways, both at work and elsewhere. Fifty-six percent of employed women reported partners harassing them at work by phone or in person; 21 percent said their partners "frequently" harassed them at work. Under the family violence amendment to the 1996 welfare law, states can refer victims of domestic violence to paid counseling and supportive programs and grant them waivers of such requirements as time limits, residency, child support enforcement cooperation rules and family cap provisions. Nineteen states have adopted many of these policies. Still, many states did not even mention domestic violence in their program plans in the first five years of reform.

More Work Hours Will Not End Poverty

Now the Bush administration is ready to double the original work rule, slash training and ignore continued shortfalls in child care and social action grants. State policies have already erased the exemption for women with young children. They are compelled to take any job—frequently low-pay work with no benefits and are then on their own.

We now know—through numerous studies funded by universities, foundations and even the federal government—what was not clear even two years ago [in 2003]: although former recipients are working more than ever before, their poverty has not significantly diminished, and their deprivation has in many instances increased. "One-third to one-half of welfare leavers reports serious economic struggles in finding food," according to Pamela Loprest, an Urban Institute economist who specializes in this field. "Almost 40 percent report problems in paying rent, and while welfare leavers have jobs similar to those of low-income mothers, leavers are less likely to have employer-based health insurance." In a study of those who left welfare within the first five years of reform. Loprest found that roughly 33 percent had to cut the size of their meals or skip meals altogether. Thirty-nine percent reported being unable to pay rent, mortgage or utility bills. Now, several years later amid a weak economy, Loprest has concluded from newer research that the employment of welfare leavers is declining, and that more of them are returning to TANF or simply abandoning public aid as a resource. "The early employment success of welfare reform is moderating," she concludes.

In the boom times of the 1990's it was relatively easy for policy makers to claim success. Today, even skilled workers take cuts in pay or benefits to hold on to employment. In this economic climate, critics say, tough work rules for typically less skilled TANF recipients are tantamount to denial of public aid.

> *"Welfare reform reduced welfare dependency, but not as much as suggested by the political rhetoric."*

Welfare Reform Has Not Gone Far Enough

Douglas J. Besharov

In the following viewpoint, Douglas J. Besharov argues that the welfare reform legislation of 1996 did help reduce the number of Americans on federal assistance but that a lot of dependency still exists in terms of food stamps, Supplemental Security Income, and other aid programs. In addition, Besharov contends that states are abetting the dependency problem by sheltering welfare recipients in state-run programs rather than forcing them to comply with the stricter welfare-to-work requirements of federal programs, which shows that the reforms did not go far enough. Douglas J. Besharov is a lawyer serving as a visiting professor at the University of Maryland's School of Public Policy. He is also a resident scholar at the American Enterprise Institute, a conservative think tank.

Douglas J. Besharov, "End Welfare Lite as We Know It," *New York Times*, August 15, 2006, p. A19. Copyright © 1997 by The New York Times Company. Reprinted with permission.

As you read, consider the following questions:

1. What two "realities" does Besharov say have convinced Republicans and Democrats that welfare reform has been a success?

2. Why does Besharov believe that the drop in caseloads may be an inaccurate representation of the commonly accepted interpretation of welfare's success?

3. According to the author, why has public and political concern about dependency largely disappeared?

It's been nearly 10 years since President Bill Clinton signed the landmark 1996 welfare reform law. The anniversary has been the occasion for various news stories and opinion pieces, most of them praising the law's success in reducing welfare dependency.

And it's true: welfare caseloads have fallen an astounding 60 percent since reform efforts began. But even as a strong supporter of welfare reform, I find it difficult to muster unqualified enthusiasm for the law and how it has been carried out.

In the years immediately before the law's passage, welfare dependency seemed out of control. From 1989 to 1994, for example, caseloads rose 34 percent. Analysts argued over how much to blame the weak economy; worsening social problems, primarily out-of-wedlock births and drug addiction; and lax agency administration. But few claimed that another 1.3 million people on welfare was a good thing.

Responding to the growing concern, [Bill] Clinton campaigned for president on a promise to "end welfare as we know it." But he had in mind something far different from what the Republicans handed him in 1996. Nevertheless, he signed the legislation that ended the welfare entitlement and gave states wide discretion, as long as they put 50 percent of recipients in work-related activities and imposed a five-year limit on financial aid.

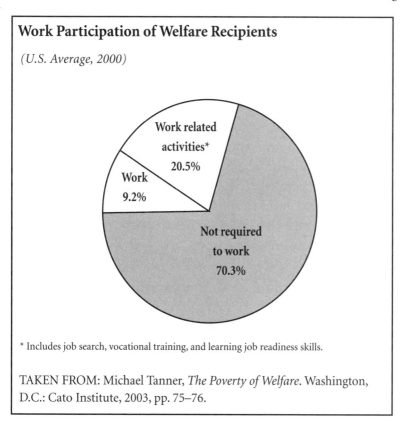

Work Participation of Welfare Recipients

(U.S. Average, 2000)

Work related activities* 20.5%

Work 9.2%

Not required to work 70.3%

* Includes job search, vocational training, and learning job readiness skills.

TAKEN FROM: Michael Tanner, *The Poverty of Welfare*. Washington, D.C.: Cato Institute, 2003, pp. 75–76.

Many feared a social calamity. But in the years since, although researchers have strived mightily, they've found only small pockets of additional hardship. Even better, the earnings of most single mothers actually rose.

Mixed Results

These twin realities—decreased caseloads and little sign of serious additional hardship—are why both Republicans and Democrats think welfare reform has been a success.

But the results are more mixed. Caseloads fell, yet they did so seemingly regardless of what actions the states took. They fell in states with strong work-first requirements, and those without them; in states with mandatory work programs, and those without them; in states with job training programs, and those without them; and in states with generous child care subsidies, and those without them.

In fact, the consensus among academic researchers is that it took more than welfare reform to end welfare as we knew it. If one looks at all the studies, the most reasonable conclusion is that although welfare reform was an important factor in caseload reduction—accounting for 25 percent to 35 percent of the decline—the strong economy was probably more important (35 percent to 45 percent). Expanded aid to low-income, working families, primarily through the Earned Income Tax Credit, was almost as important (20 percent to 30 percent).

What's more, the best estimates are that only about 40 percent to 50 percent of mothers who left welfare have steady, full-time jobs. Another 15 percent or so work part time. According to surveys in various states, these mothers are earning about $8 an hour. That's about $16,000 a year for full-time employment. It is their story that the supporters of welfare reform celebrate, but $16,000 is not a lot of money, especially for a mother with two children.

Some Still Survive on Handouts

What about the other 50 percent of families who left welfare? Well, some mothers did not "need" welfare, perhaps because they were living with parents or a boyfriend, and some left because of intense pressure from caseworkers. More troubling, about a quarter of those who leave welfare return to the program, with many cycling in and out as they face temporary ups and downs.

In addition, when they're off welfare, some of these families survive only because they still receive government assistance—through food stamps (an average of more than $2,500), the Women, Infants and Children program (about $1,800 for infants and new mothers), Supplemental Security Income (an average of over $6,500), or housing aid (an average of $6,000).

Their children also qualify for Medicaid. In reality, these families are still on welfare because they are still receiving benefits and not working—call it "welfare lite."

So, yes, welfare reform reduced welfare dependency, but not as much as suggested by the political rhetoric, and a great deal of dependency is now diffused and hidden within larger social welfare programs.

As a result, public and political concern about dependency has largely disappeared.

The tougher work and participation requirements added in [the 2006] reauthorization of the law could help states address the deeper needs of welfare families. But many states are already planning to avoid these new strictures with various administrative gimmicks, like placing the most troubled and disorganized families in state-financed programs where federal rules do not apply. This would only further obscure the high levels of continuing dependency.

For now, welfare reform deserves only two cheers. Not bad for a historic change in policy, but not good enough for us to be even close to satisfied.

| "Poverty and hunger among single mothers and their children have declined."

Welfare Reform Has Helped Poor Single Mothers

Scott Winship and Christopher Jencks

Opponents of welfare reform were wrong in their predictions that reform measures would lead to welfare recipients sinking deeper into poverty, assert Scott Winship and Christopher Jencks in the following viewpoint. According to the authors, reform policies have been successful, especially in reducing poverty rates among disadvantaged mothers and children. Winship and Jencks contend that—contrary to opponents' expectations—welfare reform has brought single mothers into the workforce and has increased their incomes. Scott Winship is a fellow at the Wiener Center for Social Policy at Harvard University. Christopher Jencks is a professor of social policy at Harvard.

As you read, consider the following questions:

1. What measure of economic well-being did Winship and Jencks use to determine how single mothers were faring after welfare reform?

Scott Winship and Christopher Jencks, "Welfare Reform Worked—Don't Fix It," *Christian Science Monitor*, July 1, 2004. Reproduced by permission of the authors.

2. Besides welfare-to-work reforms, what other government policies do the authors say have benefited the security of single mothers and their children?

3. According to Winship and Jencks, why should the government not try to bring more women off the welfare rolls by tightening welfare reform policies?

When President [Bill] Clinton signed welfare reform into law in 1996, many observers predicted a sharp increase in poverty among single mothers and their children. Some social welfare advocates worried that single mothers would be unable to find work, or that moving from welfare to work would boost their income while decreasing their material standard of living.

For example: A single mother might replace her $550 monthly welfare and food stamps with $800 per month from a $6-an-hour job, yet incur $650 monthly expenses for child- and healthcare.

As the welfare rolls fell to the lowest levels in 40 years, we counted ourselves among the concerned. But our recently completed study of 25,000 single-mother families in the post-welfare reform era surprised us. Our findings disproved the theory that welfare reform would increase hardship. Instead, poverty and hunger among single mothers and their children have declined, even taking into account the negative impacts of the 2001 recession.

Our research cannot prove that welfare reform was solely responsible for the improvement in living standards. But it does reveal an important lesson for Congress as it seeks to re-authorize federal welfare reform legislation [in 2004]: Don't fix what ain't broke.

Looking at the Statistics

Determining how single mothers fared in the wake of welfare reform is complicated. The official poverty rate for these families declined from 43 percent in 1996 to 33 percent in 2000.

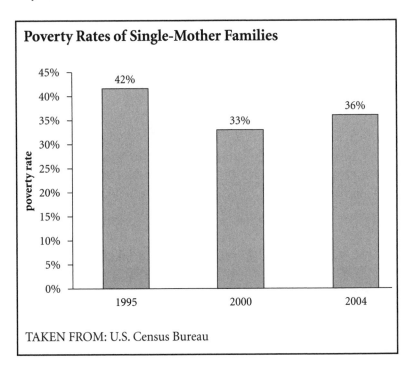

Poverty Rates of Single-Mother Families

TAKEN FROM: U.S. Census Bureau

As single mothers moved from welfare to work, their expenses for childcare, healthcare, and transportation often did increase. That's why we'd expected that welfare reform might have actually increased hardship among single mothers and their children, despite the income gains that pushed many of them above the official poverty line.

So to bypass the shortcomings of the official poverty rate as a measure of hardship, we instead examined changes in single mothers' ability to put food on the table. These measures ranged from the relatively common (whether or not a family's monthly budget ever required them to stretch their food supply) to the severe (whether a child ever went hungry for an entire day).

Our analysis of nearly 50 of these measures revealed that food problems among single-mother families consistently declined between 1995 and 2000, when the economy was expanding. Food problems increased between 2000 and 2002, during the brief recession and "jobless recovery" that followed. But by the end of 2002, single-mother families were still significantly better off than before welfare reform.

Single Mothers vs. Economic Downturns

From the early 1960s to the mid-1990s, economic expansions reduced poverty more among two-parent families than among single-mother families, and recessions harmed two-parent families more. This history is consistent with the opposing accounts of welfare as a poverty trap and a safety net: During booms, single mothers did not benefit from economic growth as much as they might have, but during busts they were shielded from rising unemployment.

But since the 1996 welfare reforms, the opposite pattern has prevailed: Until joblessness began increasing in 2000, hardship declined among single-mother families at a faster rate than among two-parent families; since then hardship has worsened at a slightly faster rate among single mothers.

Welfare reform and other policy changes that made work pay—such as the Earned Income Tax Credit, a higher minimum wage, and expanded childcare subsidies—ensured that single mothers gained more from the 1990s boom than they otherwise would have. Without these policy changes, economic growth would have had a more modest impact. The example of the late 1990s shows—contrary to the fears of liberals—that when policy "sticks" are accompanied by policy "carrots," legislators can simultaneously promote work and improve the living standards of single-mother families.

But it doesn't follow that it is now time to adopt the even tougher policies advocated by conservatives. The proposals before Congress attempt to move more welfare recipients into the workforce, and more quickly. If they succeed and do not provide sufficient work supports, the beneficial outcomes of the 1990s may not follow. This is of particular concern because the most employable women receiving welfare have already left the rolls, and the women who remain are likely to have low skill levels, poor health, sick children, and other barriers to work.

The lesson of the 1990s is that "work promotion plus work supports" can reduce poverty, but the question of how to help those who cannot find work—but face a five-year limit on federal benefits—remains unanswered.

Welfare reform was the product of compromise among both Democrats and Republicans, and it clearly has succeeded. Rather than make substantial changes of uncertain wisdom, we believe that Congress should reauthorize welfare reform along the lines of the 1996 legislation.

> *"Welfare reform was effective in getting more mothers to work, but not at making jobs work for low-wage mothers."*

Welfare Reform Has Not Helped Poor Single Mothers

Randy Albelda and Heather Boushey

Randy Albelda is a professor of economics at the University of Massachusetts in Boston. Heather Boushey is a senior economist at the Center for Economic and Policy Research, an organization promoting public education and professional research on national issues. The two authors state in the following viewpoint that welfare reform has not greatly benefited single mothers. Although many single-income welfare recipients moved into the job market, they have been mainly securing low-wage positions, Albelda and Boushey maintain. Furthermore, the authors contend that instead of breaking free of poverty, these single mothers now struggle with a lack of affordable child care, no health insurance, and many other problems faced by low-wage workers.

As you read, consider the following questions:

1. According to Albelda and Boushey, what percent of working single mothers report having employer-sponsored health care?

Randy Albelda and Heather Boushey, "From Welfare to Poverty," TomPaine.com, August 23, 2006. Reproduced by permission.

2. In the authors' view, how does low-wage employment create a "running in place" dilemma for welfare recipients?

3. Why do the authors believe the drastic drop in the number of families using welfare benefits is not a favorable sign?

This week [August 20–26, 2006] marks the 10th anniversary of the Personal Responsibility and Work Opportunity Reconciliation Act—commonly known as "welfare reform." The much hailed legislation abolished a cornerstone of the New Deal known as the Aid to Families with Dependent Children program, which was criticized for discouraging work. But 10 years later, we know that the program Congress put in its place—Temporary Assistance to Needy Families—encouraged work, but many remain in poverty and struggle to make ends meet.

Since welfare reform was passed, poor women have moved into jobs in record numbers. In 1996, more than half (54 percent) of low-income mothers with children under 6 years old were in the labor force. By 2002, that share jumped to over two-thirds (67 percent).

Minimum-Wage Work

But, the workplace has not adapted to the needs of the millions of new working single mothers. Studies of people leaving welfare consistently find that the wages of those leaving welfare average between $7 and $8 per hour, which are above the minimum wage but leave families close to or even below the poverty threshold. Further, most people found jobs that do not offer the kinds of benefits middle- and upper-class workers take for granted. Only about half of those leaving welfare report having employer-sponsored health insurance and no more than half had paid sick leave or pension coverage. Most do not have access to paid maternity/paternity or family leave and many do not even have access to unpaid leave.

In short, welfare reform was effective in getting more mothers to work, but not at making jobs work for low-wage mothers.

And, don't be fooled by the higher employment numbers into thinking that welfare reform eliminated poverty. Around the time of welfare reform's passage, Congress increased some of the benefits of working—raising the minimum wage and expanding the Earned Income Tax Credit in 1996, and creating the Child Health Insurance Program in 1997. Yet it has not significantly expanded benefits in recent years. Rather, as states struggled to balance their budgets in the early 2000s, many work-support programs have been cut. Meanwhile, the real value of the minimum wage is lower today than it was when welfare reform passed, and so far Congress has resisted raising it at every turn.

Facing the Trials of Working Poverty

By definition, welfare recipients are virtually all single-parent families and they now face the same problems faced by millions of low-income working families: not enough time and not enough income. For working parents, gainful employment requires not only a good job, but also reliable child care. While the wages of most parents leaving welfare are relatively low, child care costs remain high—more expensive than attending the state university in most states—and subsidized slots continue to be elusive.

For many families, moving to work has meant become "working poor," rather than "welfare poor." Work supports are available for some low-income workers, but evidence indicates that the percentage of eligible families receiving food stamps, earned income tax credits, housing assistance or child care vouchers is quite small relative to the need. Those lucky enough to access work supports find that they often phase out too rapidly, as each rise in income reduces benefit levels. Thus,

Education Suffers Under Work-First Policies

It has been a hard slog for educationally ambitious single mothers receiving public assistance since welfare was reformed in 1996. Even though states have preserved access to job training or college in varying degrees, it's gotten much more difficult for women in these programs: confusion over the new rules ushered in by the '96 reforms, the aggressively work-first attitude of welfare caseworkers, and stricter work-hour minimums have taken a toll.

A recent study reported a 46 percent drop in enrollment of welfare recipients in 15 Massachusetts community colleges between 1995 and 1997, for example. The enrollment of welfare recipients in the City University of New York dropped 77 percent, according to a 2001 study.

Amy De Paul, "Hello, Minimum Wage," AlterNet, *April 7, 2005. www.alternet.org.*

employment creates the "running in place" dilemma: Every additional dollar earned means close to a dollar lost in benefits.

Not Serving Those in Need

And, those finding jobs are the lucky ones. While the poverty rate has fallen dramatically since 1996, welfare caseloads have fallen even more. Between 1996 and 2004, the poverty rate for single mothers fell from 42 to 36 percent, a 14.3 percent decline, but the percentage of families using welfare fell by close to 60 percent, meaning that far fewer poor families are being served by welfare. Families who face enormous barriers to employment still need cash assistance, especially when family circumstances preclude a single parent from holding any job or a full-time job.

Nobody liked the old welfare system. It provided disincentives to employment, treated people poorly, and didn't provide enough income to support a family.

But, the current system isn't working very well, either. Too many families struggle too hard in a country that has enormous wealth. Ten years later, many low-income working families are wondering when we will insist that work should work for families—that jobs pay enough to afford the basics, that they come with health care and access to paid sick leave, and that every parent has access to safe, affordable and enriching child care for their children while they're at work.

> *"While the number of welfare recipients has been more than halved, the number of working poor families continues to grow."*

Welfare Reform Does Not Address Poverty

John Cranford

John Cranford is a columnist for CQ Weekly, *a publication that records and comments on congressional activity. In the following viewpoint, Cranford states that the 2006 reauthorization of the 1996 welfare reform law offered lawmakers a chance to move beyond measuring the policy's success in terms of reduced welfare caseloads and instead enact new reforms to help those who have left the welfare system and joined the ranks of the working poor. Unfortunately, according to Cranford, politicians seem uninterested in addressing the problems of the working poor and are unlikely to fund child care programs or balance work requirements with the desire of poor people to pursue educational opportunities. Cranford contends that without providing these supports, current and former welfare recipients will simply remain at the bottom of the economic ladder.*

As you read, consider the following questions:

1. In what year did the 1996 welfare reform law formally expire, as Cranford notes?
2. How many American working families lived on less than a poverty-level income in 2003, according to the author?
3. In Cranford's view, what three important welfare issues get the "short shrift" in current government budget proposals?

If there is one huge adverse consequence of the ideological and partisan fissure that divides Capitol Hill in the early 21st century, it is the inability of lawmakers to deliberate about and to legislate Big Ideas.

That point was proved once more in the final days of December [2005], when Congress punted for the umpteenth time instead of rolling up its collective sleeves and doing something about a static welfare system that isn't doing enough to stop the rising poverty rate and narrow the gulf between the have-mores and the haven't-enoughs.

Almost without notice, Congress is a half step away from reauthorizing the landmark 1996 welfare law for five more years without taking the time to address either its shortcomings or the broader needs of impoverished Americans. Three years after the original law formally expired in October 2002—and after 12 temporary extensions—lawmakers tucked reauthorization language into a controversial deficit-cutting bill that awaits final action by the House at the end of [January 2006]. [The Deficit Reduction Act of 2005 was signed into law.]

No one praises this benighted effort. Moreover, the underlying spending-cut bill has not won the vote of a single Democrat, so partisan objections to its welfare provisions are meaningless. And those Republicans who oppose the spending-cut bill are likewise the same people who would find fault with the welfare language. The silence is deafening.

The Impact of Welfare Reform

It's been almost a decade since a Republican Congress and President Bill Clinton, a Democratic ex-governor who had firsthand experience with the old welfare system, came to a shaky agreement that it was time to replace a failed patchwork of public assistance programs with a new compact that emphasized the importance of work to the fabric of society—not to mention the economy.

Welfare as we knew it for more than 60 years was eliminated, and politicians have been congratulating themselves ever since. To be fair, the overhaul looks to be at least a modest success. The number of welfare recipients has been cut by more than half, leaving roughly 2 million households receiving what is euphemistically called Temporary Assistance for Needy Families. Dependence on government aid has been reduced, and the culture of work is being reinforced across generations. And the decidedly Republican idea of promoting marriage, responsible fatherhood and two-parent families has found adherents across the aisle [in Congress; i.e., with Democrats].

Since the 1996 law lapsed, however, there has been no serious effort to cut a bipartisan, bicameral deal that would build a bridge to the new century for the retooled welfare system enacted on Clinton's watch. In fact, the pending reauthorization has become just another exercise in cost savings. It's not aimed at poverty reduction or even the promotion of stable working families.

Ignoring Important Issues

The bill would bump up spending for child care by a small amount and add some money for programs to encourage marriage—possibly an endeavor that will prove salutary in the long run. Critics at the Center for Budget and Policy Priorities and the Center for Law and Social Policy say the legislation will penalize states and do little or nothing to help existing

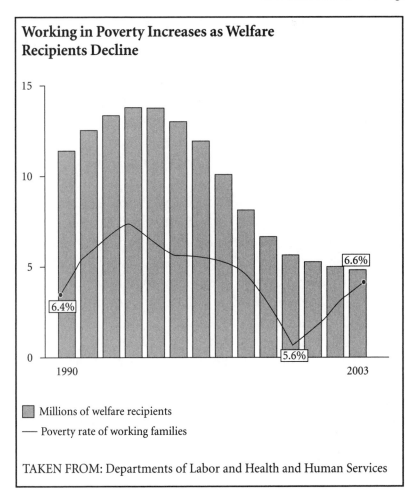

Working in Poverty Increases as Welfare Recipients Decline

- Millions of welfare recipients
- Poverty rate of working families

TAKEN FROM: Departments of Labor and Health and Human Services

families find the means to work and care for their children. The Congressional Budget Office says the cost to state governments will rise, and critics say the consequence is that states will have to choose to curtail services or pay more.

It's not just welfare parents we're talking about here: There's a whole class of working poor people in this country who barely get by. Tweaking welfare programs doesn't do very much for many of them, but the right sort of major adjustments to government thinking—and spending patterns—just might.

Official statistics on the working poor are troubling when set alongside the reluctance of Congress to discuss the problem. While the number of welfare recipients has been more than halved, the number of working poor families continues to grow. About 4.2 million families with at least one member who was working lived on less than poverty-level income in 2003, the most up-to-date Labor Department figures show. That meant 6.6 percent of all working families were poor, an increase from 5.6 percent in 2000.

Research shows that the availability of child care is critical for moving people off welfare and into the labor force. Some senators were trying to craft a bipartisan plan that would have increased child care spending by $6 billion over five years, and made it more broadly available to the working poor. That bill never made it to the floor, and the reauthorization language that sits in the not-quite-enacted spending-cut measure would increase child care spending by just $1 billion over five years. That pittance amounts to about $100 a year for each family on welfare, or $50 a year for each working poor family—assuming all were eligible—and will do very little to allow mothers or fathers to work more hours and put more money in their pockets, the ostensible goal of the new welfare regime.

Child care isn't the only issue that needs to be addressed: Job training and education also get short shrift. It's still possible that the latest welfare reauthorization will die if enough House Republicans reject the spending-cut bill. If that happens, lawmakers can go back to the drawing board on welfare.

> *"Many policy-makers and scholars still think of Temporary Assistance as 'welfare' . . . but our research establishes that this is simply no longer accurate."*

Temporary Assistance Programs Are Not Welfare

Margy Waller and Shawn Fremstad

In the following viewpoint, Margy Waller and Shawn Fremstad caution that government assistance in the post-welfare-reform era should not be confused with outdated practices of disbursing large amounts of money to the unemployed. Instead, the authors assert that modern temporary assistance programs mainly provide supports—such as child care benefits and tax credits—for low-income workers. In this way, according to Waller and Fremstad, temporary assistance is more akin to employment benefits than to cash handouts. Margy Waller is a director at the Center for Community Change, a social service organization in Washington, D.C. Shawn Fremstad is a member of Inclusion, a progressive think tank, and a social and economic adviser to several nonprofit organizations.

Margy Waller and Shawn Fremstad, "It's Not Welfare Anymore," *The American Prospect*, August 22, 2006. Reproduced with permission from *The American Prospect*, 11 Beacon Street, Suite 1120, Boston, MA 02108.

As you read, consider the following questions:

1. What two reforms (in 1993 and 1996) do the authors consider the most significant in creating true welfare reform?

2. According to Waller and Fremstad, what fraction of temporary assistance grants do states spend on cash assistance?

3. Why do the authors insist that it is important to change the conservative-supported image of welfare as dependence?

Many people are celebrating today, August 22, [2006] as the 10th anniversary of "welfare reform." While it's true that President [Bill] Clinton signed the law eliminating the previous program, Aid to Families with Dependent Children, and establishing Temporary Assistance for Needy Families block grants on this date in 1996, that was hardly the first effort to rewrite the book on welfare as we knew it. Both Congress and the states began expanding work-based reforms years earlier, and much of what now goes by the name of welfare reform took place prior to the implementation of the 1996 law. Moreover, our research, published recently by the Brookings Institution, finds that "welfare" is an inapt description of the policies adopted in the last decade [1996–2006].

To better reflect today's reality, welfare reform should be shorthand for the policy shift toward providing employment benefits to low-wage workers. Key components of this shift include reimbursement for work expenses like child care and transportation, health insurance when employers fail to provide affordable options, and policies that boost low wages, including the minimum wage and the Earned Income Tax Credit (EITC).

Social conservatives love to conflate welfare reform with the 1996 law and cite it as the turning point in our national domestic policy. They fail to credit the Democratic-led efforts predating it and laying the groundwork for its early, if mixed, success. For example, one of the most important reforms came with the 1993 expansion of the Earned Income Tax Credit. Another important policy lever was congressional passage and enactment in 1996 of a federal minimum wage hike.

Moreover, the conservative "pat on the back" for the 1996 law is belied by this reality: Almost half of the much-heralded decline in cash assistance caseloads occurred after the EITC expansion—and *before* implementation of the Temporary Assistance grants.

Viewed this way, 2006 marks a much more mature anniversary of welfare reform. Still, it is an opportune moment to focus specifically on today's Temporary Assistance in the context of broader changes.

Welfare Now Resembles Work Benefits

Many policy-makers and scholars still think of Temporary Assistance as "welfare"—a program for people who have little or no connection to the world of work. But our research establishes that this is simply no longer accurate. Instead, today's Temporary Assistance bears more resemblance to employment benefits like unemployment insurance and the Earned Income Tax Credit.

We analyzed how state officials spent their Temporary Assistance dollars, choosing to "follow the money" in order to assess priorities after states were granted new authority to set their own goals and fund services.

We found that state officials have gone from spending most of their Temporary Assistance money on cash benefits to spending it increasingly on an array of work supports and services. Moreover, the beneficiaries include a great number of parents in low-wage jobs who do not receive cash assistance at all. In fact, states on average use only about a third of their Temporary Assistance funds to provide cash assistance; instead, they provide employment benefits like those that higher-

Supports Define the New Welfare

Less well-publicized than caseload reduction and work, but as important to the long-term contours of welfare policy, the mode of welfare assistance has changed as well. TANF program benefits are defined as either "assistance" or "non-assistance." Recurring monthly welfare checks, defined by the law as "assistance," are no longer the primary source of assistance for welfare recipients. Instead, welfare-to-work programs now fund a range of social services that are defined as "non-assistance," which include short-term (less than four months in duration) childcare, job search assistance, mental health services, substance-abuse treatment, domestic violence counseling, and temporary income support intended to support work activity and help recipients overcome barriers to employment. Rather than a welfare system reliant on welfare checks, the system now uses a wide range of tools to transform individual behavior, increase work-readiness, and promote economic self-sufficiency.

Scott W. Allard, Publius: The Journal of Federalism, *2007.*

wage workers may get through their employers or the tax system: child care, transportation subsidies, and more.

Even cash assistance today bears little resemblance to welfare of old. The vast majority of those receiving cash assistance are workers: 60 percent lived in a household with at least one worker, and one-third lived in a household with a full-time worker. And Temporary Assistance lives up to its name: The typical parent receives cash assistance for only four months at a time, often when they are between jobs.

Unfortunately, policy-makers continue to think of Temporary Assistance as a welfare program. One example of this myopia is that the federal government does not even know how many families actually receive employment benefits funded with Temporary Assistance, because they only count parents getting cash assistance.

This shortsighted view puts Temporary Assistance at risk. Currently, federal law does almost nothing to require that state officials say how they are spending the funds and to set goals related to the use of funds. History shows that block-grant funds without clear programmatic goals representing broad public consensus are at risk of cuts. Temporary Assistance may fare no better if the public continues to view it as a "welfare to work" program for non-working recipients of cash assistance with little connection to the labor market.

The Importance of Changing Welfare's Image

To correct this misunderstanding and ensure funding for the future, progressive policymakers must establish clear goals and performance measures for Temporary Assistance. And they should clarify the empirical reality that Temporary Assistance is for employment benefits—designed to help make the economy work better for low-wage workers, rather than a more limited "welfare-to-work" program.

These days, conservatives are trying out a new theme: they argue that low-wage workers who get publicly funded employment benefits—things like child care and health insurance— are still depending on "welfare." We assume that conservatives are concerned about the shift in public opinion stemming from the success of these reforms. Indeed, anti-government conservatives have good reason to worry—the shift in public attitude toward support for low-wage workers could thwart their plans to undermine and, ultimately, undo these important federal benefits.

Progressive voices must combat this new effort, but we also need to articulate a positive and inclusive social policy vision making clear we're all in this together. Today, nearly one-third of our labor market comprises low-wage jobs paying barely $10 an hour, without benefits. As long as this continues, there can be no higher priority than to address the inequities faced by millions of Americans in such jobs.

Periodical Bibliography

The following articles have been selected to supplement the diverse views presented in this chapter.

America	"Welfare Reform at 10," September 25, 2006.
America	"Welfare's Unfair Work Requirement," May 19, 2003.
Stephen Baskerville	"From Welfare State to Police State," *Independent Review*, winter 2008.
Patrice Gaines	"Welfare Reform: Is It Working?" *Crisis*, January/February 2007.
Mark Greenberg	"Welfare Reform, Phase Two," *American Prospect*, September 2004.
Christopher Jencks, Joe Swingle, and Scott Winship	"Welfare Redux," *American Prospect*, March 2006.
Will Marshall	"Shrinking Underclass," *Blueprint*, July 2005.
Stephen Moore	"Time for Welfare Reform II," *National Review*, March 14, 2005.
New York Times	"Mission Unaccomplished," August 24, 2006.
Robert Rector and Christine Kim	"Welfare Reform Worked—Now Keep It Going," *Human Events*, August 28, 2006.
Robert J. Samuelson	"One 'Reform' That Worked," *Newsweek*, August 7, 2006.
John Stossel	"The Public Trough Is Bigger than Ever," *Human Events*, May 14, 2007.
Wall Street Journal	"Welfare Reform: Ten Years Later," August 26, 2006.

OPPOSING
VIEWPOINTS®
SERIES

CHAPTER 2

How Do Welfare Policies Affect Families?

Chapter Preface

As the debate over welfare reform raged in the mid-1990s, commentators often portrayed welfare recipients as idle, sexually promiscuous city dwellers getting fat and rich and raising large families off welfare handouts. Their children, according to the stereotype, would also inevitably grow up to be welfare recipients. The 1996 welfare reform legislation was intended to transform welfare into a temporary assistance program that helped move recipients into self-sufficiency by working. It was expected that the temporary nature of this assistance would discourage single-parenthood and end the cycle of dependency.

Indeed, welfare reform has had a profound effect on adults. Experts tend to agree that Temporary Assistance to Needy Families (TANF), the current welfare program, has moved unprecedented numbers of parents off the welfare rolls and into the workplace. However, the effects of TANF on the families of these welfare recipients are much less clear, even more than ten years after the program was implemented. In a report entitled "The Unfinished Business of Welfare Reform," the Child Trends research center concludes that children in TANF families generally remain disadvantaged and at risk. Furthermore, Sharon Parrott and Arloc Sherman, writing for the Center on Budget and Policy Priorities, report that "between 2000 and 2004, the number of children living in families with cash incomes below half the poverty line increased by 774,000. Over the same period, the number of children getting assistance from TANF declined."

Why many needy families choose not to avail themselves of TANF assistance is unclear. Parrott and Sherman suggest that the welfare system—which now stresses its temporary nature—does much to discourage people from seeking aid. The pair asserts, "Some states discourage families from applying for assistance, place requirements on families before their TANF application can be approved, quickly terminate assistance to families for missing appointments with caseworkers or not completing paperwork, and/or end assistance to families that do not meet work or other requirements." Whether these indictments are accurate, though, is a subject of debate.

In the following chapter, several commentators discuss the impact of welfare on children and families. Some of these authors examine the issue from the perspective that promoting healthy marriages can ensure that children do not end up in welfare-dependent families; others focus on child care and other after-the-fact realities of living in low-income families under the presiding welfare-to-work policies.

> "Marriage programs can increase child well-being and adult happiness, and reduce child poverty and welfare dependence."

Pro-Marriage Welfare Policies Help Families

Robert E. Rector and Melissa G. Pardue

Robert E. Rector is a senior domestic policy researcher and Melissa G. Pardue a former domestic policy analyst for the Heritage Foundation, a conservative Washington, D.C., think tank. According to Rector and Pardue, marriage clearly benefits both adults and children and is the foundation of a healthy society; yet, according to the authors, instead of promoting marriage, the welfare system discourages marriage and encourages parents to stay single because benefits are paid on the basis of family income. The following viewpoint was originally published to provide supporting information on a program proposed in 2002 by President George W. Bush to help welfare recipients form and sustain healthy marriages. This program was implemented in the welfare reauthorization bill passed by Congress in 2005.

As you read, consider the following questions:

1. What percentage of poor single mothers do Rector and Pardue claim would be lifted out of poverty if married to their children's father?

2. According to Rector and Pardue, how do welfare programs penalize marriage and reward single parenthood?

3. In the authors' view, how has President Bush sought to meet the original goals of the welfare reform legislation enacted in 1996?

The erosion of marriage [since the 1960s] has had large-scale negative effects on both children and adults: It lies at the heart of many of the social problems with which the government currently grapples. The beneficial effects of marriage on individuals and society are beyond reasonable dispute, and there is a broad and growing consensus that government policy should promote rather than discourage healthy marriage.

In response to these trends, President George W. Bush has proposed—as part of welfare reform reauthorization—the creation of a pilot program to promote healthy and stable marriage. Participation in the program would be strictly voluntary. Funding for the program would be small-scale: $300 million per year. This sum represents *one penny* to promote healthy marriage for every *five dollars* government currently spends to subsidize single parenthood. Moreover, this small investment today could result in potentially great savings in the future by reducing dependence on welfare and other social services.

The Importance of Marriage

Today, nearly one-third of all American children are born outside marriage. That's one out-of-wedlock birth every 35 seconds. Of those born inside marriage, a great many children will experience their parents' divorce before they reach age 18.

More than half of the children in the United States will spend all or part of their childhood in never-formed or broken families.

The collapse of marriage is the principal cause of child poverty in the United States. Children raised by never-married mothers are seven times more likely to live in poverty than children raised by their biological parents in intact marriages. Overall, approximately 80 percent of long-term child poverty in the United States occurs among children from broken or never-formed families.

It is often argued that strengthening marriage would have little impact on child poverty because absent fathers earn too little. This is not true: The typical non-married father earns $17,500 per year at the time his child is born. Some 70 percent of poor single mothers would be lifted out of poverty if they were married to their children's father. This is illustrated in Chart 1, which uses data from the Princeton Fragile Families and Child Well-being Survey—a well-known survey of couples who are unmarried at the time of a child's birth. If the mothers remain single and do not marry the fathers of their children, some 55 percent will be poor. However, if the mothers married the fathers, the poverty rate would drop to 17 percent. (This analysis is based on the fathers' actual earnings in the year before the child's birth.)

The Impact of Single-Parent Families

The growth of single-parent families has had an enormous impact on government. The welfare system for children is overwhelmingly a subsidy system for single-parent families. Some three-quarters of the aid to children—given through programs such as food stamps, Medicaid, public housing, Temporary Assistance to Needy Families (TANF), and the Earned Income Tax Credit—goes to single-parent families. Each year, government spends over $150 billion in means-tested welfare aid for single parents.

Growing up without a father in the home has harmful long-term effects on children. Compared with similar children from intact families, children raised in single-parent homes are more likely to become involved in crime, to have emotional and behavioral problems, to fail in school, to abuse drugs, and to end up on welfare as adults.

Finally, marriage also brings benefits to adults. Extensive research shows that married adults are happier, are more productive on the job, earn more, have better physical and mental health, and live longer than their unmarried counterparts. Marriage also brings safety to women: Mothers who have married are half has likely to suffer from domestic violence as are never-married mothers.

A Growing Consensus

The overwhelming evidence of the positive benefits of marriage for children, women, and men has led to a large and growing consensus that government policy should strengthen marriage—not undermine it. William Galston, former Domestic Policy Adviser in the [Bill] Clinton White House, has stated: "Marriage is an important social good, associated with an impressively broad array of positive outcomes for children and adults alike. . . . Whether American Society succeeds or fails in building a healthy marriage culture is clearly a matter of legitimate public concern."

Former Vice President Al Gore has proclaimed, "We need to be a society that lifts up the institution of marriage." Mr. Gore and his wife have concurred with the Statement of Principles of the Marriage Movement, which declares:

> We believe that America must strengthen marriages and families. . . . Strong marriages are a vital component to building strong families and raising healthy, happy, well-educated children. Fighting together against the forces that undermine family values, and creating a national culture

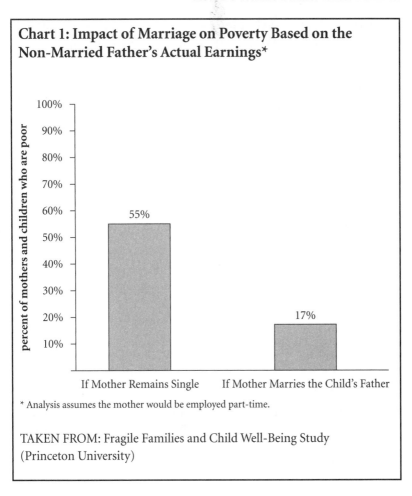

Chart 1: Impact of Marriage on Poverty Based on the Non-Married Father's Actual Earnings*

If Mother Remains Single — 55%

If Mother Marries the Child's Father — 17%

percent of mothers and children who are poor

* Analysis assumes the mother would be employed part-time.

TAKEN FROM: Fragile Families and Child Well-Being Study (Princeton University)

that nurtures and encourages marriage and good family life, must be at the heart of this great nation's public policy.

Will Marshall, of the Progressive Policy Institute, and Isabel Sawhill, widely respected welfare and family expert at the Brookings Institution, recently issued a paper entitled "Progressive Family Policy for the 21st Century." Marshall and Sawhill repudiate "the relativist myth that 'alternative family forms' were the equal of two-parent families," citing a growing body of evidence showing that—in aggregate—children do best in married, two-parent families. They argue that "a progressive family policy should encourage and reinforce married, two-parent families because they are best for children."

Welfare System Biased Against Marriage

Despite the overwhelming evidence of the benefits of marriage to families and society, the sad fact is that, for more than four decades, the welfare system has penalized and discouraged marriage. The U.S. welfare system is currently composed of more than 70 means-tested aid programs providing cash, food, housing, medical care, and social services to low-income persons. Each year, over $200 billion flows through this system to families with children. While it is widely accepted that the welfare system is biased against marriage, relatively few understand how this bias operates. Many erroneously believe that welfare programs have eligibility criteria that directly exclude married couples. This is not true.

Nevertheless, welfare programs do penalize marriage and reward single parenthood because of the inherent design of all means-tested programs. In a means-tested program, benefits are reduced as non-welfare income rises. Thus, under any means-tested system, a mother will receive greater benefits if she remains single than she would if she were married to a working husband. Welfare not only serves as a substitute for a husband, but it actually penalizes marriage because a low-income couple will experience a significant drop in combined income if they marry.

For example: A typical single mother on Temporary Assistance to Needy Families receives a combined welfare package of various means-tested aid benefits worth about $14,000 per year. Suppose the father of her children has a low-wage job paying $16,000 per year. If the mother and father remain unmarried, they will have a combined income of $30,000 ($14,000 from welfare and $16,000 from earnings). However, if the couple marries, the father's earnings will be counted against the mother's welfare eligibility. Welfare benefits will be eliminated (or cut dramatically), and the couple's combined income will fall substantially. Thus, means-tested welfare programs do not penalize marriage *per se* but, instead, implicitly penalize marriage to an employed man with earnings. The practical effect is to significantly discourage marriage among low-income couples.

This anti-marriage discrimination is inherent in all means-tested aid programs, including TANF, food stamps, public housing, Medicaid, and the Women, Infants, and Children (WIC) food program. The only way to eliminate the anti-marriage bias from welfare entirely would be to make all mothers eligible for these programs regardless of whether they are married and regardless of their husbands' earnings. Structured in this way, the welfare system would be marriage-neutral: It would neither reward nor penalize marriage.

Such across-the-board change, however, would cost tens of billions of dollars. A more feasible strategy would be to experiment by selectively reducing welfare's anti-marriage incentives to determine which penalties have the biggest behavioral impact. This approach is incorporated in the President's Healthy Marriage Initiative.

Healthy Marriage Initiative

In recognition of the widespread benefits of marriage to individuals and society, the federal welfare reform legislation enacted in 1996 set forth clear goals: to increase the number of two-parent families and to reduce out-of-wedlock childbearing. Regrettably, in the years since this reform, most states have done very little to advance these objectives directly. Out of more than $100 billion in federal TANF funds disbursed over the past seven years, only about $20 million—a miniscule 0.02 percent—has been spent on promoting marriage.

Recognizing this shortcoming, President Bush has sought to meet the original goals of welfare reform by proposing a new model program to promote healthy marriage as a part of welfare reauthorization. The proposed program would seek to increase healthy marriage by providing individuals and couples with:

- Accurate information on the value of marriage in the lives of men, women, and children;

- Marriage-skills education that will enable couples to reduce conflict and increase the happiness and longevity of their relationship; and

- Experimental reductions in the financial penalties against marriage that are currently contained in all federal welfare programs.

All participation in the President's marriage program would be voluntary. The initiative would utilize existing marriage-skills education programs that have proven effective in decreasing conflict and increasing happiness and stability among couples. These programs have also been shown to be effective in reducing domestic violence. The pro-marriage initiative would not merely seek to increase marriage rates among target couples, but also would provide ongoing support to help at-risk couples maintain healthy marriages over time. . . .

The primary focus of marriage programs would be preventative—not reparative. The programs would seek to prevent the isolation and poverty of welfare mothers by intervening at an early point before a pattern of broken relationships and welfare dependence had emerged. By fostering better life decisions and stronger relationship skills, marriage programs can increase child well-being and adult happiness, and reduce child poverty and welfare dependence.

| *"There is no evidence that marriage-promotion efforts actually work."*

Pro-Marriage Welfare Policies Do Not Help Families

Sharon Lerner

The Healthy Marriage Initiative, a proposal attached to the welfare legislation before Congress in 2004, was designed to encourage low-income parents to get married. In the following viewpoint, Sharon Lerner argues that this initiative is based on faulty reasoning; just because married people tend to be wealthier, healthier, and better-educated than singles, it does not mean that being poor, unwell, and uneducated can be cured by getting married. Unfortunately, according to the author, the initiative promotes marriage in its most traditional, most religious sense and ignores the obstacles to marriage caused by poverty and domestic violence. Lerner, a senior fellow at the Center for New York City Affairs at New School University, is writing a book about the lack of public support for American women.

As you read, consider the following questions:

1. According to Lerner, what two parts can the Bush marriage strategy be broken into?

2. What are the two cultural forces specifically listed by the author that have caused marriage rates to drop since 1970?

3. In Sara McLanahan's view, as stated by Lerner, what kinds of services would one-third of unmarried new parents need before marrying?

Taken the wrong way, a correlation can be a dangerous thing. Consider the relationship between marriage and well-being. There's much undisputed evidence that married people are, on average, wealthier, healthier and better educated than their single counterparts. Even the novice student of statistics will tell you that association does not mean causation—that being poor, unwell and uneducated is as likely to discourage marriage as the other way around. Nevertheless, the notion that tying the knot can alleviate poverty and bring about positive social change has become the central justification for the [George W.] Bush Administration's push for low-income women to get and stay married.

If the Administration is really concerned about poverty and other social problems it claims are caused by divorce and singleness, why not tackle those ills directly? Instead, what the Administration calls the "Healthy Marriage Initiative" is an array of programs that promote the institution in its narrowest sense. While debate has centered on the proposal attached to the stalled welfare bill, [passed by Congress in late 2005] which would allot $1.6 billion toward marriage-related projects [through 2009] the federal government has already committed more than $90 million to marriage-related projects since 2001, according to the Center for Law and Social Policy. (The funds have been drawn from such diverse—and inappropriate—sources as the Office of Refugee Resettlement, the Administration for Native Americans and the Developmental Disabilities Program.)

Why Low-Income People Do Not Get Married

The Bush marriage strategy can be broken into two parts: efforts to encourage single people to marry and those aimed at keeping married couples together. The theory underlying the first category, which includes pro-marriage media blitzes featuring billboards, posters, calendars and pamphlets as well as premarital classes for high school students, singles and unmarried couples, is that explaining the benefits of marriage will nudge people to the altar. The assumption seems to be that the targets of these campaigns somehow forgot about the institution—or that they don't know enough to desire it.

But it turns out most low-income people already want to get married. Perhaps the most illuminating insight into why they don't comes from the Fragile Families study, an ongoing, in-depth investigation of the relationships of more than 3,700 mostly low-income, unmarried couples in twenty US cities that began in 1998. According to these researchers, led by Princeton sociology professor Sara McLanahan, 86 percent of the unmarried mothers and 91 percent of the unmarried fathers who were living together around the time of their child's birth said they wanted to get married. Yet by the end of the year, only 15 percent of these couples had.

Administration officials seized on these findings, taking them to mean that marriage-education efforts need to reach poor couples during this "magic window" after birth. But inadvertently or not, they missed the key point: Most couples in the study didn't follow through with their plans to marry because they faced daunting and sometimes insuperable obstacles, such as infidelity and drug abuse.

Poverty also seems to make people feel less entitled to marry. As one father in the survey put it, marriage means "not living from check to check." Thus, since he was still scraping bottom, he wasn't ready for it. "There's an identity associated with marriage that they don't feel they can achieve," McLanahan says of her interviewees. (Ironically, romantic ideas about weddings—the limos, cakes and gowns of bridal magazines—seem to stand in the way of marriage in this context. Many in the study said they were holding off until they could afford a big wedding bash.)

Underlying the anxiety around marriage identity is real poverty that eats away at people's abilities to be supportive parents and life partners. And while the chicken-egg conundrum of money and marriage comes up here, the Fragile Families study offers evidence that income facilitates marriage; an increase of one dollar per hour in men's wages in the study increased the odds they'd marry by 5 percent. Men who earned $25,000 or more in the past year had more than double the rates of marriage of those who didn't.

Shortcomings of the Marriage Strategy

Given the stresses of poverty, one might predict that direct income support would improve relationships. In fact, one of the few government efforts to have a documented effect on marital relationships is the Minnesota Family Investment Program, which increased employment and cash supports for long-term welfare recipients. According to MDRC, a nonprofit research organization that evaluated the Minnesota program, unmarried cohabiting couples who participated in it were almost 38 percent more likely to marry, and participants who were already married were less likely to divorce. Another income support program, the Wisconsin W-2 study, had a similarly positive effect on relationships. Yet the Bush Administration has said its marriage money cannot be used toward any efforts—whether income support like these, drug treatment or employment assistance programs—that do not directly address the issue of marriage.

Policy-makers crafting the marriage plan have also evaded the inconvenient reality of domestic violence, which at any given time affects between 15 and 25 percent of the welfare

Benefits of Marriage Not Available to All

In its *Loving v. Virginia* ruling, the U.S. Supreme Court declared marriage is "one of the basic civil rights of man," and the freedom to marry is "essential to the orderly pursuit of happiness." But "basic civil rights" and "the orderly pursuit of happiness" mean nothing to [George W.] Bush or the Christian Right.

Families staying together are without doubt important. Families often do need resources to help achieve that goal. It is also absolutely true that parents—and their families—benefit physically, financially, mentally and emotionally from a healthy marriage. But Bush and the Christian Right care only about some parents and some families.

Gay and lesbian couples and their real-world American families—that include hundreds of thousands if not millions of children—are excluded from the benefits of the Healthy Marriage Initiative paid for with *their* tax money because the federal government—based on perverted, malignant religious ideology—denies them the civil right to a civil marriage.

Mel Seesholtz,
Online Journal, *January 6, 2006.*

caseload. Relationship violence should, of course, be a deterrent to marriage. Distressingly, though, mothers in the Fragile Families study who were victims of violence weren't any less likely to marry their partners. Advocates are concerned that, in their zeal for marriage, marriage educators may overlook domestic violence. Or, by offering financial incentives to marry, as several do, programs will encourage women to get or stay in violent relationships.

Some of the state-based marriage programs, including the Oklahoma Marriage Initiative, have welcomed the advice of domestic violence experts on the curriculum for marriage classes and allowed them to train people leading the state's workshops. But, while Administration officials have repeatedly said they don't want to push women into violent relationships, they have given money to many programs that do not have such provisions to protect against domestic violence, and the pending marriage initiative attached to the welfare bill does not require programs to include them.

Using Marriage to Reduce Poverty

It's true that, if the government were somehow able to increase marriage rates just by encouraging and educating people without dealing directly with these hurdles, the poverty rate would register a slight decrease. When researchers conducted a statistical simulation of marriage, matching single mothers and unmarried men who are similar in age, education and race, they found that, if marriages were increased to 1970 rates, just by combining incomes the poverty rate would drop from 13.0 percent to 9.5 percent. Of course, pooling resources can make life easier financially (though many of the people being encouraged to marry already do). Yet no one knows how to get couples to marry; there is no evidence that marriage-promotion efforts actually work. Moreover, such programs ignore the overlapping cultural forces—including the increasing economic independence of women and gay liberation—that caused marriage rates to drop in the first place.

There is some evidence that efforts to help married people stay together can be effective. Studies have shown that certain workshops, counseling sessions and classes now being considered or funded by the government can improve communication between married couples and cut down on marital discord. But so far, this research reflects the experience only of the mostly middle-class participants who have sought out these programs and not that of the poor people the current marriage effort is now targeting.

The difference is critical. Various projects are under way to adapt programs to this new population, translating books and manuals into Spanish and producing written materials for people with lower reading levels, according to the Administration. But as even Wade Horn, the Department of Health and Human Services' Assistant Secretary for Children and Families and architect of the marriage initiative, admits, "It's much more complicated than just taking the drawing of the Lexus in the driveway and putting it in front of an apartment complex." Indeed. By focusing just on marriage, rather than on the problems of poverty and violence, Horn and his cohorts are unlikely to succeed in preserving many marriages in low-income populations.

Programs encouraging low-income couples to get married are similarly limited by the overwhelming problems of the populations they target. According to McLanahan of the Fragile Families study, one-third of unmarried new parents would need social services such as drug or mental-health treatment before marrying, while circumstances, such as incarceration or a couple not being romantically involved, put marriage out of the question for another third.

Based on Flimsy Research

Nevertheless, the Administration is eagerly pushing ahead, willing to recruit any bit of research to its cause, no matter how flimsy or biased. Or so it would seem, judging from a May [2004] press conference that touted an evaluation of a community marriage initiative run by Marriage Savers, a Christian group that employs clergy to prevent divorce.

The report, which was co-written by Stan Weed, concluded that the group's efforts resulted in a decline in divorce rates in certain counties. (Before conducting the study, Weed received $46,737 from Marriage Savers, according to his 2002 tax return, though the group says it was just passing on money for the evaluation from a Justice Department grant. The conservative Heritage Foundation, which strongly supports the marriage-promotion initiative, helped procure the funding for the study.) But even Weed, a conservative Mormon researcher known to be supportive of abstinence and marriage programs, concluded that the drop in divorce rates was "modest" and could be the result of forces other than the Marriage Savers program. Still, Horn seemed to regard the study as a strong defense of the entire marriage plan. "Critics of the Health Marriage Initiative have charged that we don't know how to help more couples to build lifelong marriages or to reduce the likelihood that half of new marriages will end in divorce," he said at the press conference. "This pioneering research by Dr. Stan Weed and colleagues proves them wrong."

And despite the Administration's rhetorical emphasis on "healthy marriage," the study took the view that the reduction of divorce is a positive outcome, regardless of the quality of the marriage. Religion is clearly at least part of the reason that Horn, who was himself a board member of Marriage Savers before taking a government position, and others seem so eager to promote the institution at any cost. Marriage Savers is openly church-based, and Michael McManus, president of the organization, sees marriage in biblical terms. "Couples often live together as a way to test the relationship. However, both Scripture and sociology suggest they are embracing evil," Mc-Manus writes on the group's website. Through his program, "churches help couples test their relationship while holding onto good and avoiding the evil."

Marriage Savers is just one of several religious groups promoting marriage, and the Bush Administration would clearly like the number to be higher. A March 29 [2004] statement from the Administration plugs its latest priorities on the welfare bill, including the expansion of "charitable choice" provisions, which would allow more faith-based organizations to get marriage grants through the bill. Revealingly, the policy statement also opposes any increase in funding for childcare.

Taken together with the Administration's support of a constitutional amendment against gay marriage (without even a halfhearted attempt to explain why the institution wouldn't bestow the same supposed benefits on same-sex couples), the limit on childcare funding and the emphasis on religion help answer at least one of the looming questions about the marriage initiative: The Administration isn't focusing its policies on poverty and social problems because they're not the point. Marriage is—in its most traditional, most religious sense, in which women stay at home with children and are financially dependent on their husbands. Rooted in politics rather than research, the Bush marriage initiative is symbolic policy that aims to appear "compassionate," even as it skirts the real problems of poverty and turns back the clock on women's and gay liberation.

| "'Welfare-to-work' policy is likely to be fundamentally ineffective in . . . reducing poverty among young mothers or even in reducing the rates of . . . single motherhood."

Welfare Policies Do Not Affect Unwed Parenting Rates

Christine Carter McLaughlin and Kristin Luker

Christine Carter McLaughlin is a researcher in sociology, and Kristin Luker is a professor of sociology at the University of California–Berkeley. In the following viewpoint, McLaughlin and Luker suggest that policy makers are using panic over an epidemic of teenage pregnancy to drive welfare reform. Such claims have no basis, the authors note, because teenage pregnancy rates are at historic lows. According to McLaughlin and Luker, teenage pregnancy has become a touchstone for moralists who fear that unwed mothers are a symptom of society's permissiveness and decay. Furthermore, the authors argue, out-of-wedlock births are the result, and not the source, of the impoverished conditions that some young single women experience and thus cannot be reduced by welfare reform.

Christine Carter McLaughlin and Kristin Luker, "Young Single Mothers and 'Welfare Reform' in the US," *When Children Become Parents: Welfare State Responses to Teenage Pregnancy*, Bristol, UK: Policy Press, 2006. Copyright © Anne Daguerre and Corinne Nativel 2006. Reproduced by permission.

As you read, consider the following questions:

1. What percentage of young women with less than a high school education give birth before the age of twenty, as stated by the authors?
2. For some girls, what do pregnancy and childbearing represent, in the authors' view?
3. According to McLaughlin and Luker, what is the Findings section of the 1996 welfare reform bill about?

Adolescent birth rates in the US reached their peak in the post-war Baby Boom, reaching a level of 96 births per 1,000 women under age 20 in 1957. Importantly, most of those births were to married parents. Teenage birth rates in the US have ranged from 63 per 1,000 in 1920, to 82 in 1950, to 89 in 1960. They went back down to 68 in 1970, and ironically were at 56 per 1,000 in 1975 when the 'epidemic' was declared—and they continued to fall from there to 53 in 1980. They rose to 63 in 1990, but went back down again to 49 per 1,000 in 2000. Pregnancy rates are also declining, from 99 per 1,000 women under 20 in 1973 to 86 in 2000 (see Table 1). The teenage pregnancy rate is down 29% since its most recent peak in 1990. . . .

Actual Proportions of the Epidemic

Despite considerable concern at the political level about the teenage pregnancy rate, pregnancy, abortion and birth rates among adolescents are all in decline. The US is not experiencing an epidemic of teenage parenthood. The rhetoric of 'children having children' is a cover for moral concern about sexually active unwed women and single mothers—not teenage mothers. However, just because teenage pregnancy is not the problem it is portrayed to be does not mean that it is not a real problem for teenagers who become pregnant. Importantly, current 'welfare-to-work' policy is likely to be fundamentally ineffective in bringing about positive change—say, in reducing poverty among young mothers or even in reducing the rates of sexually active unwed women or the rates of single motherhood—because it is not connected to the motivational roots of the *actual* problem. Without a better understanding of the women for whom government support is designed, and the social and economic context of their lives, there can be no useful understanding of adolescent motherhood and no basis for preventing it.

Young women who are poor and otherwise disadvantaged are far more likely to have children as teenagers than are their better-off peers. Forty per cent of poor women in the US have children before they are 20 years old, while only 7% of those in high economic status groups do. Eighteen per cent of poor mothers give birth by the age of 18, while only 3% of their wealthier counterparts do. Thirty-four per cent of those with less than a high school education give birth before they are 18, compared to 3% of those with some college education. And while 7% of young women with some college education give birth before the age of 20 in the US, a stunning 66% of those with less than a high school education do so. . . .

Poverty Among Teen Mothers

Poverty and disadvantage bring increased social and environmental risk factors such as failing schools, dangerous neighbourhoods and violent families. Judith Musick, who studied disadvantaged youth and adolescent mothers extensively, documents how the lives of adolescent girls raised in poverty are different in every dimension relative to those raised in middle-class families and neighbourhoods. Disadvantaged 'girls frequently have grown up in damaged and damaging family situations where the basic developmental foundation has been poorly laid or is lacking altogether. . . . Their external supports and their opportunities to find alternative models of coping are fewer and far less adequate.' Taught that education will not help them out of poverty by the experiences of the people

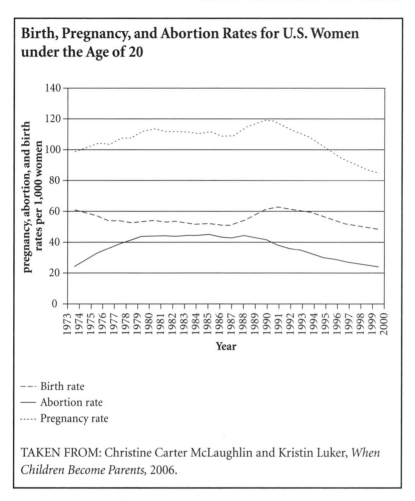

Birth, Pregnancy, and Abortion Rates for U.S. Women under the Age of 20

--- Birth rate
— Abortion rate
····· Pregnancy rate

TAKEN FROM: Christine Carter McLaughlin and Kristin Luker, *When Children Become Parents,* 2006.

around them, the life options for disadvantaged youth are limited in number and offer little hope of life outside of poverty. American public schools in low-income neighbourhoods are notoriously troubled places, offering teenagers little hope or inspiration for a better life.

Adolescent mothers in the US are not just likely to be suffering from a poverty of occupational and educational opportunities, however. They are also more likely than their better-off peers to be experiencing what Elaine Bell Kaplan calls a 'poverty of relationships'. Like Kaplan, Musick has found that disadvantaged teenagers have often experienced 'frequent separations from primary attachment figures in early life, which leave residues of vulnerability to threats of abandonment'. In her ethnography of poor adolescent teenagers, Kaplan found that there was often little 'consistent, useful guidance from significant adults and few positive alternate role models'. Although teenage girls are at a point in their development where they need affirmation by and connection to others, 'many feel unloved by their mothers, ignored by their schools, and rejected by their fathers and boyfriends'. This absence of familial and other forms of social support in the lives of teenage mothers helps us to understand why they get pregnant and want to keep their children. Sexual activity creates at least the illusion of connection to a male figure. Fathering a baby has the potential to draw that male father into a girl's life. Pregnancy also draws attention to girls who are otherwise often isolated. One teenage mother wrote in her journal, 'I like it when people notice I'm having a baby. It gives me a good feeling inside and makes me feel important'. Pregnancy and childbearing represents, for some girls, the most obvious way for them to try to create the loving and attentive family they crave.

Poor Adult Role Models

Poverty also brings with it a dramatically increased risk of sexual abuse, which sadly becomes *the* significant form of sexual socialisation for many young women—and which also explains why some girls are more likely to become pregnant as adolescents. A study conducted by the Ounce of Prevention Fund found that 61% of its US sample of 445 black, white and Hispanic pregnant and parenting teens had been sexually abused. Sixty-five per cent of these victims reported abuse by more than one perpetrator, and three quarters of them had been abused more than once. . . .

The pervasive poverty—of economic and emotional resources and of relationships—and sexual abuse in the lives of young unwed mothers reframes popular perception of single motherhood from an active choice motivated by welfare assistance to one that represents a highly constrained choice among limited options. As [social historian] Linda Gordon notes [in her book *Woman's Body, Woman's Right: A Social History of Birth Control in America*], many of these women find themselves 'falling into motherhood'. The future is particularly bleak for many teenage mothers. Sexual abuse and lack of developmentally appropriate nurturance can stunt cognitive and academic development, setting even smart and talented teenagers up for failure in school. Parents often offer little in the way of hopeful role modelling. Parental employment in impoverished neighbourhoods usually has little prospects. One girl in Kaplan's study explained that most of the women she knew in her mother's generation were on welfare, cleaned houses, or worked in the fast food industry for the minimum wage—not something to look forward to. Moreover, mothers who themselves gave birth as teenagers model behaviour their daughters are likely to replicate: seeking gratification through early motherhood. . . .

Welfare Policy and Unwed Sexuality

Because of the vagaries of the US federal system, states varied in the level of benefits they provided to needy mothers prior to the 1996 PRWORA [Personal Responsibility and Work Opportunity Reconciliation Act, signed into law by President Bill Clinton]. In addition, the real value of welfare benefits declined over time as inflation increased. Thus, two kinds of natural experiments—over time and across states—have led scholars to conclude that welfare has very modest effects, if any, on fertility rates. For white teenagers in particular, states with higher rates of benefits may have lower 'legitimation' rates, that is, rates of marriage among already pregnant couples. But the 'moral panic' over teenage pregnancy and out-of-wedlock births had already set the stage for a union of fiscal and social conservatives to put an end to almost 60 years of social provision. Although there is considerable evidence that President Bill Clinton imagined replacing welfare with more generous efforts to help needy individuals enter the paid workforce, the bill that eventuated from his campaign promise to 'end welfare as we know it' mixes together moral and social anxiety about sexuality, changing gender relations, and new family forms.

In the US system, Congress often inserts a section in new legislation called 'Findings'.... Most interestingly, when read carefully, the Findings section of the 1996 welfare reform bill makes clear that the new legislation is only indirectly about government financial assistance or work, two items readers could be forgiven for thinking are most central to questions of poverty and its alleviation. Rather, the Findings section is about sex, teenagers, and single motherhood. The key point here is that the Findings section shifted the debate at a national level from a debate about poverty and jobs to one about marriage and unwed sexuality. . . .

Confusing Effect and Cause

The first two items in the Findings section of the welfare reform bill note that 'marriage is the foundation of a successful society', and 'marriage is an essential institution of a successful society which promotes the interests of children'. The Findings section then moves from marriage to a consideration of how it is related to the need for welfare reform: 89% of children receiving [pre–welfare reform aid payments] are in homes where no father is present; this in turn is due to an increased propensity for unmarried women to get pregnant; that the rates for younger women are increasing more quickly than the rates for older women; and that non-marital births are associated with negative outcomes for women, for children and for society. Almost imperceptibly, the categories of pregnancy, unwed births and teenage births became collapsed into one another, and the resulting amalgam of teenage unwed births becomes identified as the *source* of poverty rather than as a *result* of it.

On a simple statistical level, the arguments made in the Findings section are undeniably true. Single-parent families, which are most often single-mother families, are poorer than two-parent families; this holds true even in nations with generous social provision. While not always teenagers, single mothers are, of course, young: rates of unmarried births are increasing faster among young women than older women, mostly because younger women have more of their reproductive years ahead of them and are still building their (possibly unmarried) families.

Moreover, the 'problem of children having children' is seen by Congress as a willful refusal among some women to marry rather than the simple but unfortunate fact that many poor young women cannot find men who will commit to them through marriage, or cannot find men who are able, most often through no fault of their own, to earn enough money to pull them out of poverty. Welfare is seen as the problem, not the solution, in that it is assumed to motivate or at least enable unmarried childbearing. The Findings section of the Bill, and the sections that follow, make clear that the national panic driving welfare reform is about a rise in *single* parenting rather than *teenage* parenting. Time limits on welfare are designed to make alternatives to marriage less reliable and more daunting, and a national commitment to abstinence is designed to make marriage more alluring.

"The deficiency of child care under TANF [is] the big failure of the program."

Welfare Provides Inadequate Child Care for Needy Families

Josefina Figueira-McDonough

The welfare reform enacted in 1996 placed new emphasis on work requirements, thrusting many parents who had previously been at home caring for children into the workplace. In the following viewpoint, former Arizona State University professor of social work Josefina Figueira-McDonough examines how the welfare system has responded to the increased demands for child-care services generated by the new welfare policies. According to the author, despite major increases in funding for child-care subsidies, a large proportion of eligible children do not receive them, and many low-wage working parents are also faced with an inadequate supply of child-care providers.

As you read, consider the following questions:

1. In this viewpoint, how many children are reported by the author as receiving child-care subsidies during the period 1996–2001?

2. What are two of the bureaucratic obstacles to low-income working families' receiving child-care subsidies, in the author's view?

3. According to Figueira-McDonough, what positive effect do child-care subsidies have on employment, both for welfare recipients and those off welfare?

A s TANF [(Temporary Assistance for Needy Families) became law in 1996], the obligation of adult recipients to work became unavoidable. This crucial change triggered a corollary need for child care and raised, in turn, the importance of the government's role in providing it through the program. The 1996 welfare reform combined federal programs of child care subsidies under the Child Care Development Fund (CCDF). In accordance with the move toward devolution, states could exercise considerable discretion regarding eligibility and benefits. They could use TANF money for child care, either directly or by transferring up to 30 percent of TANF money to CCDF, and they could add their own funds as well.

Barriers to Receiving Child-Care Subsidies

Child care subsidies burgeoned rapidly from 1996 to 2000, and state TANF funds grew to exceed the primary CCDF funding. The number of children receiving subsidies nearly doubled during this period, reaching 1.9 million. The subsidies are generally provided through vouchers set at 75 percent of child care costs in the community of the recipient. The guidelines for the voucher program are parental choice, work requirement, and the priority given to families leaving welfare for work. Copayments, income eligibility, and reimbursements vary from state to state.

Despite the increase in funding, a large proportion of low-income working families are not getting subsidies. In 13 of the 16 states studied by [the Institute for Women's Policy Research], 30 percent or more of eligible children were not get-

---

Table 1: Percent of Monthly Income Spent on Child Care by Employed Mothers of Children Under 15

Income

Less than $1,500	24.4%
$1,500 to $2,999	13.0%
$3,000 to $4,999	10.5%
$4,500 and over	5.8%

TAKEN FROM: Julia Overturf Johnson, "Who's Minding the Kids? Child Care Arrangements: Winter 2002," United States Census Bureau Current Population Reports, October 2005. www.census.gov.

---

ting subsidies. Because the funds were insufficient to meet demand, states rationed services in several ways. In an expanded countrywide assessment, it was found that in nearly all (47) states, eligibility levels were lowered. More than half (35) of the states excluded low-income working parents who were not receiving welfare. Thirteen states required a minimum of work hours for eligibility. All states limited outreach efforts, leaving many low-income working parents in the dark about the subsidies.

To these problems, a number of the usual bureaucratic obstacles were added. Intakes were frozen and waiting lists created. Priorities were set so that only certain categories of applicants were served. Applications were made very complex, requiring lengthy paperwork and office visits, forcing parents to take time from work.

Hard Choices in Child-Care Services

Other barriers stem from the inadequacy of child care centers in the areas where low-income families live and the high fees charged by these centers, relative to family budgets. [Table 1] shows that as income declines, the proportion of child care costs goes up. Forty-two percent of families who left welfare for low-skilled, low-wage jobs paid an average of $232 a month for child care in 1999. Another hindrance is that the tight schedules that many low-income women encounter at work reduce their child care options.

This mismatch between child care funding and demand worsened in 2001, when many states entered budget crises. By then, the states served 18 percent—1 in 7—of federally eligible children. The situation has deteriorated further, as 13 states decreased their investment in child care assistance in 2002. In one of these states, California, over 200,000 eligible children are on the waiting list. The costs of services and restrictions on these services seriously jeopardize poor working women trying to keep up their work commitments, and lack of access to quality child care compounds the problem.

Parents who get child care subsidies in the amount calculated for services in their neighborhood are faced with hard choices. Nearly all live in poor neighborhoods, with limited choices, where child care services may be unable to adapt to the mothers' work schedules. Faced with these hassles, almost 30 percent of parents with subsidies have recoursed to unregulated child care.

Regulated group care and child centers have to meet health and safety standards even if they cannot provide quality care. The states might devote some of their child care money to improve these services, but there is no evidence that they have engaged in interventions, recommended by child care experts, such as lower child-adult ratios and improved staff training.

The Benefits of Quality Child Care

Two considerations make the deficiency of child care under TANF the big failure of the program. The first concerns the sheer number of children in need of this service. According to 2001 TANF statistics, half of the parents receiving assistance have children under 6 years of age. Second, good child care offers the best chance to break the intergenerational cycle of poverty. A growing number of studies indicate that the initial years of life are critical for children's long-run social, emotional, and cognitive development. Intervention in early childhood can help overcome obstacles created by poverty.

Evidence from the Perry School in Ypsilanti, Michigan, the North Carolina Abecedarian Project, and the Chicago Child-Parent Program confirm this. All three programs developed preschool programs for children living in poverty. By age 20, those who had been enrolled in any of these experiments had significantly higher rates of secondary school completion and lower rates of juvenile delinquency than the control groups. The Chicago Program calculated that good public child care would result in a return to society of $7 for every dollar spent on the program, calculating both tax revenues from future economic activity and savings in remedial education and crime control costs. In sum, good child care might in fact be an effective tool in breaking the generational cycle of poverty.

Other research shows a strong connection between the availability of child care and the participation of mothers in the workforce. Child care subsidies increase the duration of employment, both for welfare recipients and those off welfare. Forty percent of those receiving this type of assistance were more likely to stay employed for at least 2 years than were those without. The impact goes still higher (60 percent) for former welfare recipients, and the benefits show up in the quality and stability of child care.

We know, then, that child care has two important effects: It makes it easier for low-income women to work in a sustained manner, and it helps give their children a better future.

Some commentators point out that, at least for low-income workers, child care should not be left to the market, which by definition responds to competitive pressures and profit. Many OECD (Organization for Economic Cooperation and Development) countries—Denmark, England, Finland, New Zealand, Scotland, Spain, and Sweden—have made the care of preschool children a universal right. The delay of the United

States in responding to the balance of benefits/costs in child care may reflect an unresolved schizophrenia. Two ideals—the self-sufficiency/work ethic and the traditional nuclear family ethic, with its gendered functions—pull against each other.

> *"It's time for us to restore children's needs to their proper place at the center of the [welfare] debate."*

The Welfare Debate Should Focus on Children

Nancy K. Cauthen

Sociologist Nancy K. Cauthen, deputy director of the National Center for Children in Poverty at Columbia University, examines welfare reform from a historical perspective in the following viewpoint. According to Cauthen, welfare was originally created to help keep mothers out of the labor force so that they could care for their children, but social change and expansion of the welfare rolls in later decades made employment the focus of the welfare debate. Now, the author argues, the neglected needs of low-income children must resume their place as the most important welfare-related issue.

As you read, consider the following questions:

1. What was the focus of the alternative welfare policy that Cauthen states was considered but rejected when welfare was first created?

Nancy K. Cauthen, "Looking Forward, Looking Back: Reflections on the 10th Anniversary of Welfare Reform," National Center for Children in Poverty, Mailman School of Public Health, Columbia University, August 2006. www.nccp.org. Reproduced by permission.

2. According to the author, how did the primary causes of single motherhood shift from those envisioned by the original creators of ADC?

3. How much do parents who leave welfare for employment typically earn, in Cauthen's view?

As we approach the 10-year anniversary [in August 2006] of the signing of the Personal Responsibility and Work Opportunity Reconciliation Act (PRWORA), commonly referred to as "welfare reform," pundits are rushing to declare the effort either an unqualified success or an utter disaster. Despite the hype, most of us know that the truth lies somewhere in between. There have been undeniable successes, yet significant policy challenges remain. Welfare reform is not over.

The Consensus About Work

Perhaps the greatest achievement of the 1996 reform effort was the bipartisan consensus on work: the primary goal of the newly created Temporary Assistance for Needy Families (TANF) program was to require adult recipients to work or prepare for work as a condition for receiving benefits. Despite many disagreements about specifics (for now, I'm placing aside concerns about the newest federal requirements), these pale in comparison to the accomplishment of placing work at the center of temporary assistance policy. This profound development rectified a fundamental flaw in the original federal welfare program, Aid to Dependent Children (ADC).

When the program was created in 1935 as part of the Social Security Act, most mothers were not employed. In fact, the program was designed to keep mothers out of the labor force. Its intended recipients were children in families where the father had died, deserted the family, or was unable to work because of disability. By providing cash assistance, policymakers hoped to allow these single mothers to remain home to care for their children. At the time, employed single mothers risked having their children removed from the home.

What most people don't realize is that an alternative approach was considered but rejected. The policy that prevailed focused on ensuring that children had maternal care at home. The alternative proposal did this as well, but it also emphasized the lack of income from employment. It would have provided aid to children living in homes "in which there is no adult person, other than one needed to care for the child or children, who is able to work and provide the family with a reasonable subsistence compatible with decency and health." In short, the failed proposal linked the family's need for assistance to the absence of income from employment rather than to family structure.

By highlighting children's need for nurturing care as well as their need for income from a parent's employment, the alternative might have resulted in a more flexible policy—for example, one in which family and employment policies were coordinated, rather than inhabiting different worlds. It might have led to a more constructive path for ADC. We will, of course, never know.

The Politics of Welfare

The creators of ADC could not have imagined the radical economic and social transformations that would render their policy obsolete. The primary causes of single motherhood soon began to shift, from death and desertion to divorce, separation, and childbearing outside of marriage. At the same time, as Southern agriculture mechanized, large numbers of impoverished African Americans moved from the rural South to Northeastern and Midwestern cities in search of work. Over time, more mothers entered the labor force and social attitudes about women working outside the home began to change.

Social policy changed as well. The Old-Age Insurance program, commonly known as Social Security, added a survivor's benefit and eventually one for disability. Spouses and children of workers who died or who became disabled could turn to Social Security instead of ADC. As of 1974, means-tested benefits for the indigent elderly and disabled who did not qualify for Social Security benefits were provided through Supplemental Security Income (SSI). In short, more generous programs gradually siphoned off the most politically sympathetic families from ADC, which went from serving a "pitied" population to one that was perceived as "undeserving."

None of this satisfactorily explains why aid recipients were pilloried by politicians and the press as early as 1950. Political speeches and magazine articles lambasted recipients, blaming public aid for causing moral laxity and laziness and for encouraging fraud—despite the lack of evidence for any of these claims. Initially, most of the wrath was directed at unemployed men who had deserted their wives and children; the exemplars were typically white. But as AFDC (in 1962, ADC was renamed Aid to Families with Dependent Children, or AFDC) grew in size, especially after caseloads exploded in the 1970s, politicians, pundits, and the public increasingly directed their anger at black, never-married mothers, despite the fact that the largest group of recipients was white children. Welfare politics have rarely been only about welfare.

Media Sensationalism

Given the vast amount of attention that policymakers and the media have devoted to welfare over the last 50 years, ordinary citizens can be forgiven for thinking that it's the nation's largest social program. This is, of course, patently false. In 2005, 4.5 million individuals (of whom only about a million were adults) received TANF benefits, in comparison to the 48 million who received Social Security checks. Annual government spending on TANF for basic support is around $10 billion,

Percent of Children Living in Poor Households with an Adult Working Full-Time in 2003

Alabama	30.8	Montana	34.1
Alaska	14.3	Nebraska	20.7
Arizona	33.6	Nevada	28.2
Arkansas	28.4	New Hampshire	14.7
California	28.1	New Jersey	17.6
Colorado	25.2	New Mexico	40.8
Connecticut	10.8	New York	25.7
Delaware	22.6	North Carolina	29.4
District of Columbia	30.9	North Dakota	24.6
Florida	29.3	Ohio	21.2
Georgia	25.2	Oklahoma	32.2
Hawaii	23.7	Oregon	25.1
Idaho	33.3	Pennsylvania	18.8
Illinois	25.5	Rhode Island	22.0
Indiana	23.5	South Carolina	26.7
Iowa	19.5	South Dakota	22.1
Kansas	21.7	Tennessee	26.7
Kentucky	30.9	Texas	39.6
Louisiana	38.3	Utah	25.1
Maine	19.7	Vermont	15.0
Maryland	15.5	Virginia	18.1
Massachusetts	16.9	Washington	22.4
Michigan	22.0	West Virginia	23.9
Minnesota	13.7	Wisconsin	20.9
Mississippi	35.7	Wyoming	26.6
Missouri	22.5	U.S.	26.0

TAKEN FROM: Current Population Survey March Supplement, 2004.

while Social Security costs now exceed $500 billion. More children benefit from Social Security (because a parent has died or become disabled, or because an adult household member is eligible) than receive TANF. It would be helpful if the media would take more responsibility for placing these programs in perspective.

Fortunately, mainstream media provide far less blatantly sensationalistic coverage of welfare than in years past. But they continue to stereotype both TANF recipients as well as the poor in general as black. Moreover, the media have a penchant for offering in-depth portrayals of African-American single mothers with five or six children, despite their statistical rarity; more than 90 percent of poor single mothers have only one, two, or three children.

I have asked reporters why they profile atypical families. Their responses are always similar: something along the lines of "it makes for a more compelling story." I always respond that this contributes to misinformation about the poor and reinforces stereotypes about blacks and about welfare. They typically say "interesting point" and publish their stories anyway. To be fair, the media do not create these stereotypes—the stereotypes persist because they resonate with views that Americans already hold. But their perpetuation has been an obstacle to sensible policy—not to mention damaging to delicate race relations.

How to Improve Welfare

Given the status of welfare policy 10 years after the 1996 reforms, I would like to offer three major policy strategies for improving the well-being of low-income children and their parents.

Make Work Pay. The consensus about work has led to a more constructive debate regarding welfare than in decades past. But we know that employment, by itself, is not always enough to improve a family's financial condition. Parents who exit welfare for employment typically earn poverty-level wages ($8.00 an hour or so). Research is clear that children are no better off if their families leave welfare for work unless family income increases.

Stricter work requirements and regulations that make it more difficult for states to recognize education as a legitimate work preparation activity simply exacerbate the problem. What's needed are strategies that make work pay—raise the minimum wage, expand earned income tax credits, and provide greater access to work support benefits such as child care assistance and health insurance. Yes, these options are costly, but they are investments toward helping families achieve economic self-sufficiency and will pay off in the long run.

Policymakers need to focus on all low-wage workers raising children, not just those on welfare. TANF recipients comprise only a tiny fraction of the families who can't make ends meet because of low pay. More than 30 million Americans—a quarter of the U.S. labor force—work in jobs that pay poverty-level wages and that provide few prospects for advancement and income growth.

Address Needs of the Most Vulnerable. Practitioners, along with many state-level policymakers, have argued for years that the next major challenge for welfare reform is to figure out how to assist families that have multiple barriers to employment. These barriers include limited education; problems with mental illness, substance abuse, and domestic violence; criminal records; health problems; and/or chronically ill or deeply troubled children. Although they comprise a minority of recipients who enter the welfare system, such families often remain for long periods because immediate and steady employment is simply not realistic. Policymakers in Washington have yet to seriously address the needs of these families, leaving the states to grapple with the problems—which the new rules will only make worse by limiting the time recipients can devote to treatment for mental illness or drug addiction, or to remedial education.

Unable to cope with the requirements, many of these families simply leave the welfare rolls, and we have little information about what happens to them. This can be especially dangerous for children. The most vulnerable families also are the ones who are the most likely to be cited for child welfare violations, such as neglect. When such families are on TANF, they are more visible to government authorities in a position to address signs of trouble. By not assisting these very needy families, we consign their children to a bleak future

Place the Welfare of Children at the Center of the Welfare Debate. If it's true that the way a nation treats its children says a lot about that nation, the United States has a lot of work to do (and not just in terms of welfare, but that's another essay). Looking at welfare historically reminds us that concerns about children were the original impetus for ADC. We know from research that children have not been universally helped or harmed by welfare reform. For example, we know that welfare policies that increase employment and income can improve school achievement among elementary school children. At the same time, there's evidence that adolescents' school progress may be harmed when their parents leave welfare for work, perhaps because these older children take on additional responsibilities (such as caring for younger siblings) or perhaps because they receive less supervision.

One of the casualties of welfare reform's narrow preoccupation with employment is that policymakers have ignored the fact that all parents have another critically important responsibility—the care and nurturance of their children. The needs of children have disappeared from the public discourse about welfare, and it's time for us to restore children's needs to their proper place at the center of the debate.

Periodical Bibliography

The following articles have been selected to supplement the diverse views presented in this chapter.

William C. Bell	"Tough Lessons in Child Welfare Reform," *New York Times*, January 21, 2003.
CQ Researcher	"Did Recent Reforms Help Needy Families?" September 7, 2007.
Erik Eckholm	"Mothers Skimp as States Take Child Support," *New York Times*, December 1, 2007.
Carmen L. Golay	"Women Under Threat," *off our backs*, May/June 2003.
Heidi Goldberg	"Many Families Miss Out on Crucial Food Stamp Benefits," *Nation's Cities Weekly*, November 20, 2006.
Ayelish McGarvey	"Women and Children Last," *American Prospect*, September 2004.
Marvin Olasky	"Fathers Are Vital for True Welfare Reform," *Human Events*, March 6, 2006.
Robert Pear	"A Welfare-to-Work Study Finds No Harm to Children," *New York Times*, March 7, 2003.
Policy & Practice	"More Uninsured After Welfare Reform," June 2006.
Robert Rector	"How Not to Be Poor," *National Review*, October 24, 2005.
Gabriel Thompson	"The Good-Behavior Bribe," *New York*, November 5, 2007.
Rebecca Winters	"A New Marriage Proposal," *Time*, November 8, 2004.
Mortimer B. Zuckerman	"Family-Unfriendly Policies," *U.S. News & World Report*, October 15, 2007.

CHAPTER 3

How Can the Welfare System Discourage Dependence?

Chapter Preface

When the government inaugurated the Personal Responsibility and Work Opportunity Reconciliation Act (PRWORA) in 1996, it redirected cash-assistance welfare funds into block grants given to the states under the Temporary Assistance for Needy Families program. At the same time it mandated these grants, the PRWORA cut $55 billion in federal funding for several other state welfare programs. In part, the cuts were achieved by restricting eligibility for the Food Stamp Program and placing a time limit on how long an able-bodied adult could receive food stamps. Legal immigrants who had not become citizens or had worked in the country for ten years were among those who lost food stamp benefits as well as other forms of public assistance such as Medicaid. Young adults with disabilities were another group to feel the PRWORA cuts. Most lost their Medicaid and Supplemental Security Income benefits at age 18 because the new guidelines reassessed them under the stricter criteria placed upon disabled adults. Together, these eligibility restrictions helped account for the $55 billion in cuts.

Critics of welfare reform have argued that this decline in public services has hindered the elimination of poverty in the United States. Depriving immigrants and other needy families of food stamps and financial supports, they contend, keeps them from climbing out of deprivation. Some observers have noted that the savings gained from these cuts were not matched by other methods of budget pinching. Writing for the Center on Budget and Policy Priorities, Sharon Parrott and Arloc Sherman point out, "Only a tiny amount of the cuts reflected reductions in administrative costs or savings resulting from anti-fraud measures; virtually all took financial support away from low-income individuals." Activist organizations have taken up the harshness of some of the support cuts and won modest reversals. In 1998, for example, food stamp privileges were restored to immigrant children and some disabled and elderly legal immigrants who had been in the country before the passage of the PRWORA.

Such political manipulation, however, makes welfare reform proponents bristle. To them, restoring benefits defeats the purpose of reform. Senator Jon Kyl, a Republican from Arizona, argues, "If the number of people on welfare increases, each state will have fewer surplus federal resources to provide such benefits as childcare and transportation assistance. Additionally, an expanding number of beneficiaries, as opposed to the decline in recent years, will eventually result in increasing the amount of taxpayer resources dedicated to this program." Kyl and other defenders of PRWORA insist that the welfare safety net is already strong enough to support almost everyone for a limited time, but that reversing reform trends will lead back to the problematic system of dependence that characterized the longstanding welfare state.

In the following chapter, commentators on both sides of the debate examine some of the controversial issues that still haunt welfare reform. Those who champion this unprecedented legislation favor tighter controls and more restrictions to discourage dependence, while critics suggest that the policies may be so insensitive as to place thrift above the needs of individuals and families who rely on welfare services to survive.

> *"The focus [of immigration policy] needs to shift ... to reducing ... social programs and encouraging immigrants to avoid reliance upon the government dole."*

Illegal Immigrants Should Be Stopped from Draining Public Services

Rachel Alexander

Rachel Alexander is a lawyer and the coeditor of Intellectual-Conservative.com, a Web site devoted to conservative politics. In the following viewpoint, Alexander argues that illegal immigration is a major problem in the United States because illegal immigrants pay no taxes yet consume welfare resources at the taxpayers' expense. According to Alexander, border security has not stemmed the tide of illegal immigrants, so the government should focus instead on depriving them of social aid so that they will be disinclined to sneak into the country.

Rachel Alexander, "Illegal Immigration Solution Must Focus on Costs," *Intellectual Conservative*, September 10, 2005. www.intellectualconservative.com. Reproduced by permission of the author.

As you read, consider the following questions:

1. How do U.S. employers who hire illegal immigrants contribute to the burden on the nation's welfare program, in Alexander's view?
2. Before Roosevelt's New Deal reforms, why were immigrants less of a burden on the United States, according to Alexander?
3. In the author's estimate, how many illegal immigrants enter the United States each year?

Illegal immigration is rapidly becoming one of the biggest problems in society today. Former President [Bill] Clinton stated that "our borders leak like a sieve." A workable solution has proven elusive because the problem lies not so much with the addition of sheer numbers to the U.S. population, but rather with the disproportionate increase in costs to society illegal immigrants bring along. Yet the main focus of resolving the problem has been on border control, making it difficult to distinguish the two. This results in the assumption that concerns about illegal immigration stem from a desire to keep immigrants out.

This is not accurate, since U.S. law permits a significant number of legal immigrants into the country each year; approximately 480,000 family-based immigrants and 140,000 employment-based immigrants, as well as around 80,000 refugees and 20,000 immigrants seeking asylum, who may then apply to become legal permanent residents.

Handing Out Welfare to Immigrants

Unfortunately, the problem of illegal immigration is at a stalemate, since a large portion of society, led by those on the left, is reluctant to address the costs posed by illegal immigration. As the U.S. developed into a welfare state, poor illegal immigrants increasingly used a larger percentage of taxpayer dollars through reliance on government programs and use of other

The High Cost of Low Education

The best predictor of poverty and welfare dependence in modern America is education level. Given the low educational levels of most recent immigrants, we would expect them to be a greater drain on public coffers than the immigrants who came before them. Indeed this is the case. In 1997 the National Academy of Sciences (NAS) estimated that immigrant households consumed $20 billion more in public services than they paid in taxes each year. Adjusted for inflation, with the current size of the immigrant population [in 2006], this figure would be over $40 billion.

Steven Camarota,
"Immigration Is Hurting the U.S. Workers,"
June 2007. www.usbc.org.

government resources, such as law enforcement and deportation. Further, since many U.S. employers illegally hire these workers at substandard wages, they avoid collecting social security taxes from them in order to hide their existence. This results in less taxes paid by illegal immigrants for the government services they disproportionately use. Current U.S. immigration policy reflects the reality that U.S. government handouts are too easy to obtain, and so only 5,000 of 140,000 employment-based visas per year are granted to unskilled workers.

This dilemma is troubling in terms of the history of our country, which had virtually no restrictions on immigration (although resident minorities have been treated as second class citizens and slaves) until 1882, when the Asian Exclusion Acts barred Asian immigrants from citizenship or ownership of property. The Statue of Liberty, which historically greeted poor immigrants coming into New York Harbor, has the poem

"The Great Colossus" by Emma Lazarus, imprinted on it, which contains the famous words, "Give me your tired, your poor, your huddled masses, yearning to breathe free." Before FDR's [Franklin Delano Roosevelt's] New Deal established the welfare state, immigrants came to the U.S. knowing they would have to work hard in order to provide for themselves. Although there were private charitable organizations, those organizations could attach whatever restrictions they wanted to their aid, such as requiring the recipient to perform charitable work or attend church in exchange for room and board.

But since the onset of government welfare programs in the twentieth century, the number of programs and their size has gradually increased, disproportionately relative to other government spending, taking up a bigger chunk of the average taxpayer's income. In 1900, the government spent $10 billion on social welfare programs, by 1988 it was spending $980 billion. Those programs made up 12 percent of the federal budget in 1940, and increased to almost 40 percent of the budget today. Spending on welfare programs alone rose from $1.3 billion in 1940 to $18 billion in 1992, an increase from half a million welfare recipients to 13 million. There are still over 5 million people receiving welfare benefits today. The average taxpayer now pays in taxes one out of every three dollars earned. Whereas in 1940, only one out of every eight dollars earned went to taxes.

Discouraging Illegal Immigration

Paralleling the increase in social welfare spending has been an increase in illegal immigrants. Each year the population increases by approximately 485,000 illegal immigrants—although this number is disputed, with the Census Bureau placing it at around 250,000 and the Federation for Immigration Reform placing it closer to 1 million. The total number of illegal immigrants in the U.S. is estimated somewhere between 11 and

20 million, 500,000 of which live in Arizona. Almost one-third of immigrants entering the country in the 1990's were illegal.

It is all too apparent where the real problem lies—the focus needs to shift from primarily border control to reducing taxpayer funded social programs and encouraging immigrants to avoid reliance upon the government dole. Nearly 90 percent of immigrants arrive with income and social service levels less than one-tenth of those in the U.S. A *Business Week* poll found that 10% of immigrants in California were on welfare, compared to 8% of California residents. The bloated U.S. welfare state cannot continue expanding. Even without the influx of illegal immigrants, the cost of citizens dependent upon U.S. social programs is escalating out of control, as evidenced by the social security predicament. At some point, proponents of social welfare programs have to admit that it is their philosophy that is turning illegal immigration into a crisis.

| "Worries about immigrants draining public coffers in the United States are unjustified."

Illegal Immigrants Do Not Drain Public Services

Douglas S. Massey

In the following viewpoint, Douglas S. Massey, a professor of sociology and public affairs at Princeton University and the author of Beyond Smoke and Mirrors: Mexican Immigration in the Age of Economic Integration, *contends that illegal immigrants are not a burden on U.S. welfare. He claims that illegal immigrants pay taxes at high rates and do not avail themselves of most social services. Massey suggests that this reluctance to use welfare services may be due to immigrants' desires to stay out of public view in light of harsh immigration laws enacted in the late twentieth and early twenty-first centuries.*

As you read, consider the following questions:

1. As cited by Massey, what percentage of illegal Mexican aliens reported receiving welfare payments, according to the study done by the Mexican Migration Project?

Douglas S. Massey, "Illegal Immigrants: Are They Freebies or Freeloaders?" *San Diego Union-Tribune*, June 2, 2006. Reproduced by permission of the author.

2. What percentage of illegal aliens reported using hospitals in 2002, according to the study done by the Mexican Migration Project, as cited by the author?

3. In Massey's view, why are legal and illegal Mexican immigrants more likely to "contribute to U.S. public coffers rather than take from them"?

A persistent myth in the debate about illegal migration is that migrants consume public services but don't pay taxes and therefore represent a burden to American taxpayers. According to a recent ABC News/*Washington Post* poll, a third of all Americans said their biggest concern about illegal immigrants was that they "used more public services than they pay for in taxes."

Whatever one may think about the issue of illegal migration as a political or moral issue, worries about immigrants draining public coffers in the United States are unjustified. Since 1982, the Mexican Migration Project, which I co-direct, has interviewed thousands of Mexican migrants in a variety of legal statuses. Analysis of these data clearly show that illegal migrants pay taxes at high rates while using public services at low rates.

Among some 2,100 undocumented migrants surveyed by the project, for example, only 4 percent said they used food stamps on their last U.S. trip and just 3 percent said they received government welfare payments. In contrast, 60 percent said they had federal taxes withheld from their pay. Moreover, even though undocumented migrants are legally entitled to send children to U.S. public schools, only 11 percent reported doing so. Immigrants also are entitled to emergency medical care in the United States, but only 26 percent said they used a hospital on their last trip.

Falling Rates of Welfare Usage

We thus observe that a significant gap exists between the rate of tax payment and the rate of service usage among undocu-

Illegals Pay for Benefits They Cannot Enjoy

Aliens who are not self-employed have Social Security and Medicare taxes automatically withheld from their paychecks. Since undocumented workers have only fake numbers, they'll never be able to collect the benefits these taxes are meant to pay for. [In 2005], the revenues from these fake numbers—that the Social Security administration stashes in the "earnings suspense file"—added up to 10 percent of the Social Security surplus.

Shikha Dalmia, Knight-Ridder/Tribune News Service, May 1, 2006.

mented Mexican migrants, a fact that might surprise many Americans. U.S. citizens might be even more surprised to learn that this gap is widening over time in ways that are increasingly favorable to taxpayers: Rates of tax payment are increasing while rates of service usage are falling.

The usage rate for food stamps and welfare among illegal migrants has remained low at just 3 percent to 4 percent over the past two decades; but the percentage sending children to public schools fell from 12 percent during 1987–92 to just 7 percent between 1997 and 2002. Over the same period, the share using a hospital dropped from 30 percent to 20 percent. On the revenue side of the ledger, however, federal tax withholding rose from 60 percent to 67 percent.

A Chilling Effect

Some observers have labeled falling rates of service usage among undocumented migrants as reflecting a "chilling effect." For a variety of reasons, migrants are increasingly afraid to use public services. In the wake of California's Proposition

187 [reducing public services for illegal immigrants] and the 1996 Immigration and Welfare Reform Acts, immigrants got the message that while their labor might be accepted and tax payments welcomed, their consumption of social services in the United States was not appreciated. There was a growing chill in the air.

Since undocumented migrants generally have low rates of service usage, however, this chilling effect has affected documented more than undocumented migrants. From 1987 to 1992, for instance, 60 percent of legal immigrants surveyed by the Mexican Migration Project used a hospital but between 1997 and 2002 the share had fallen to 42 percent. Over the same period the percentage with children in U.S. schools fell from 35 percent to 19 percent, and food stamp usage dropped from 15 percent to 5 percent. Welfare usage remained roughly constant at 8 percent to 10 percent. Tax payments, meanwhile, rose from the already high level of 90 percent to reach 95 percent between 1997 and 2002.

Among both legal and illegal Mexican migrants, the likelihood of filing a tax return—and thus having any hope of receiving a refund—has fallen in recent years. Between 1997 and 2002, for instance, just 67 percent of legal immigrants and only 5 percent of undocumented migrants reported filing a federal tax return. In other words, all Mexican immigrants, but especially the undocumented, are likely to contribute to U.S. public coffers rather than take from them. Instead of stereotyping migrants as freeloaders, they should more accurately be seen as freebies.

I *"The problem isn't Mexicans. The problem is the welfare state."*

Ending Welfare, Not Immigration, Will Eliminate Dependence

John Semmens

In the following viewpoint, John Semmens asserts that illegal immigrants are not currently a burden on the welfare system. He claims that illegal aliens are more likely to stay away from government authorities rather than to get involved with federal or state organizations. Although illegal immigrants cannot be blamed for draining welfare, Semmens argues that the system itself should be indicted for creating dependence among those Americans who do use social services. John Semmens is an economist and a policy advisor for the Heartland Institute, a conservative nonpartisan public policy research organization.

As you read, consider the following questions:

1. In Semmens's view, why is it difficult for illegal immigrants to obtain welfare benefits?

John Semmens, "Welfare Is Problem, Not Immigration," *The Mountain Mail* (Salida, CO), August 31, 2006. Copyright © 2006 *The Mountain Mail*. Reproduced by permission of the author.

2. Why does the author allow that an influx of illegal aliens might become a reality and a potential burden on welfare?

3. What would be the economic benefit of eliminating the welfare system, according to Semmens?

One of the big arguments for tightening immigration barriers is the fear immigrants will enlarge the welfare rolls. An example of this fear was recently demonstrated in California at a hearing of the House Government Reform Committee in San Diego.

"San Diego may be the gateway to Mexico, but our taxpayers are the doormat," County Board of Supervisors Chairman Bill Horn said. "Every dollar spent on providing services to illegal immigrants or their children is a dollar that isn't used on taxpaying citizens."

The idea of people sneaking into the country to soak the American taxpayer provokes anger. To be fair, though, native-born Americans are already soaking the American taxpayer and ought to provoke a similar anger. In fact, illegal immigrants account for only a tiny minority of those currently on the welfare rolls.

Immigrants Unlikely to Use Welfare

Those who run the gauntlet of fences, guards and environmental hardships to illegally enter the United States evince a measure of enterprise that would seem to make them unlikely to seek out welfare benefits.

An illegal immigrant arriving in America is more apt to avoid contact with government authorities than to try to scam the system. The bureaucracy normally requires those applying for welfare to show a birth certificate, visa, or passport to sign up for food stamps or cash assistance. Illegals would need to steal or forge such documents if they are to game the system.

Rather than go to the trouble of trying to defraud the welfare system, illegal immigrants are more likely to proceed

Teaching Dependence

Before [the post-1965 immigrant wave], immigrants assimilated into a culture of hard work and self-reliance. Those who failed here often had to go home. Few go home today because of failure. Instead, they are taught to assimilate into a system of government reliance where failure and laziness are not punished. The post-1965 immigration wave is the first that has come once we had a welfare state in place. Unfortunately, that welfare state not only makes them less productive, it also teaches them to undermine our old culture that made America successful.

This problem is not unique to immigrants though. All American culture is being perverted by the welfare state.

Benjamin Powell,
"Immigration, Economic Growth, and the Welfare State,"
April 30, 2005. www.independent.org.

directly to vacant, entry-level, low-paying jobs. Working illegals are not a burden to the economy. They provide useful services and pay taxes to help support the government.

The worry that an influx of illegal aliens may lead to a potentially crushing welfare burden is not entirely unwarranted. There are political elements in the U.S. who view a rising welfare clientele as a key to electoral success.

Inasmuch as reforms enacted during the 1990s significantly reduced existing welfare rolls, the power base of those favoring big government has been diminished. So, while the welfare system's current drain on our economy cannot fairly be blamed on illegal immigrants, unrestrained immigration could significantly worsen this drain.

Welfare Creates Dependency

It is the welfare system that has sucked generation after generation of American citizens into the trap of dependency. The availability of government subsidies lures people away from the effort of work.

The opportunity to get compensation for drug and alcohol related disabilities lowers people's resistance to these vices. Payments to unwed mothers undermine the incentive to take precautions against unplanned pregnancies.

These evils of the welfare system predate any problems we may perceive arising from illegal immigration. The pernicious effects of the welfare system would continue to take a toll even if our borders were perfectly impervious to illegal penetration.

In short, the problem isn't Mexicans. The problem is the welfare state.

When government takes on paternal responsibility for everyone it is an open invitation to freeloaders—at home and abroad. The solution is not closing our borders. It is eliminating the practice of robbing taxpayers to provide benefits for a client underclass.

This would remove the disincentives for work inherent in the system. It would also return money to the private sector, where it could sustain more business activity and investment—providing more jobs for natives and immigrants.

Whether these clients of the welfare state are Mexicans or native-born Americans, the process of robbing taxpayers to support them is wrong. Focusing attention only on Mexican "invaders" turns the issue into one of race and nationality and obscures the moral wrong of theft.

People traversing geography in search of a better life is how the American continent was populated. There is no moral foundation for policies that attempt to close the doors so we can preserve the good life for us. There is no real us vs. them.

We are all human beings trying to survive and provide for our families. The crime is that government coercion is used to force some to take on the responsibility of providing for others.

> *"[The food stamps program] ... has all the worst features of the old pre-reform welfare, fostering ... long-term dependence."*

Restricting Food Stamps Would Discourage Dependence

Rich Lowry

Rich Lowry argues in the following viewpoint that efforts to reform the food stamp program are necessary. He states that food stamps are currently given to many who are undeserving and that unlike other welfare handouts, there is no restriction on how many years a recipient can claim food stamp benefits. According to Lowry, this is merely an example of how some features of welfare still need restricting in order to curtail dependence. Rich Lowry is an editor of the National Review *and the author of* Legacy: Paying the Price for the Clinton Years.

As you read, consider the following questions:

1. According to Lowry, welfare recipients are eligible for food stamps if their annual income is less than what percent of the poverty line?

Rich Lowry, "Poor-Mouthing the Bush Budget," *National Review Online*, February 25, 2005. Reproduced by permission.

2. As the author reports, how long have half the recipients of food stamps been collecting this benefit?

3. What percentage of food stamp aid goes to single-parent homes, according to Lowry's report of Heritage Foundation findings?

After baseball, President [George W.] Bush's favorite sport is beating up on the poor. Or so we are told by critics of [his] budget. *New York Times* hyperventilator Paul Krugman recently wrote, "It may sound shrill to describe President Bush as someone who takes food from the mouths of babes . . ." then, of course, went on to so describe him. Bush has not yet been seen swiping Gerbers from babies at any campaign event, nor does his budget effectively do the same.

Critics say Bush wants to deny food stamps to 300,000 hungry people and child care to another 300,000 deprived kids. These charges are baldly oversimplified and rather rich coming from the same people who oppose extending the most successful anti-poverty program in the past 30 years—the 1996 welfare-reform law. For many liberals, the poor apparently exist only to be a line item in the federal budget, where they should be left undisturbed by any strenuous effort to end their soul-killing dependence on government.

Enacting Needed Restrictions

The administration's budget proposes tightening up eligibility for food stamps. When the 1996 welfare reform created the Temporary Assistance for Needy Families [TANF] program, food-stamp eligibility was extended to anyone receiving any TANF-funded service. This includes activities reaching people who have earnings that exceed the traditional food-stamp eligibility requirement of a gross annual income less than 130 percent of the poverty line. According to the Office of Management and Budget, some states make anyone receiving even a TANF-funded pamphlet eligible for food stamps.

Means-Tested Programs Penalize Marriage

While it is widely accepted that welfare is biased against marriage, relatively few understand how this bias operates. Many erroneously believe that welfare programs have eligibility criteria that directly exclude married couples. This is not true.

Nevertheless, welfare programs do penalize marriage and reward single parenthood because of the inherent design of all means-tested programs. In a means-tested program such as Food Stamps, the benefits are reduced as nonwelfare income rises. Thus, under any means-tested system, a mother will receive greater benefits if she remains single than if she is married to a working husband. Welfare not only serves as a substitute for a husband, it actually penalizes marriage because a low-income couple will experience a significant drop in combined income if they marry.

Robert E. Rector,
"Reforming Food Stamps to Promote Work and Reduce Poverty and Dependence," June 27, 2001. www.heritage.org.

The administration wants to restore the old eligibility requirement. The $36 billion a year spent on food stamps would be reduced in 2006 by $57 million. If this is class warfare, it's not exactly "shock and awe."

Both food stamps and child-care spending—which the administration wants to hold steady—should properly be considered together with welfare reform and the effort to renew it.

Add Work Requirement

Food stamps itself could use reform. It has all the worst features of the old pre-reform welfare, fostering the long-term dependence of nonworking single parents. According to Robert Rector of the Heritage Foundation, half of food-stamp aid goes to recipients who have been on the program for 8.5 years or more. Of the aid that goes to families, roughly 85 percent goes to single-parent homes. Adding a work requirement to food stamps for the able-bodied could have the same catalytic effect as the 1996 welfare reform, which reduced dependence, child poverty and out-of-wedlock births.

Congressional Republicans have wanted to reauthorize and strengthen the 1996 welfare reform [since 2002], but Democrats have blocked them. Notably, Republicans have proposed spending $1 billion more [between 2005 and 2010] on child care. By blocking the bill, Democrats have therefore effectively said "no" to $200 million of additional day-care spending every year [since 2002]. Who's keeping deprived kids off day care now?

Reform Should Encourage Work

Welfare reform relates to child-care spending in another way. As the 1996 reform decreased dependence and the amount of money spent on cash welfare benefits, more funds were available to be redirected into child care. According to a Heritage Foundation analysis, federal and state spending on child care increased from $3.2 billion in 1996 to $11 billion in 2002. Two-thirds of the new spending came from funds freed up by welfare reform, in an implicit bargain that said, "We won't pay you not to work, but we will pay to support your working." . . .

Very little has been done to attack the welfare problem at its root—single parenthood—by encouraging marriage. The 1996 reform helped slow the rate of out-of-wedlock births, suggesting more effort here could have results. But realizing the necessity of strengthening welfare reform requires viewing the poor as more than a federal line item.

> *"Significantly strengthening the food stamp program would go far toward ending hunger."*

Food Stamp Benefits Should Be Expanded

Linda Bopp

In the following viewpoint, Linda Bopp states that U.S. food stamp benefits have not changed much since the 1970s. Trying to live on the meager allowance is difficult for many low-income families and other welfare recipients, she contends. Bopp advocates that Congress should expand food stamp benefits and raise allowances because the program is efficient, well-managed, and many government agencies agree that it would help end hunger in America. Linda Bopp is the executive director of the Nutrition Consortium of New York, a nonprofit organization that conducts outreach, education, and advocacy to alleviate hunger.

As you read, consider the following questions:

1. As Bopp states, the reauthorization of what bill proposed by the Department of Agriculture every five years determines food stamp allowances?

2. How many children of New York State benefit from the food stamp program, according to the author?

3. What dollar amount does Bopp hope the Senate will set as the minimum monthly individual allowance for food stamps in 2007?

N o one is feeling the effects of escalating food prices more than our neighbors who must rely on food stamps.

The food stamp program, America's first line of defense against hunger, marked its 30th anniversary on Sept. 29, [2007]. Congress has an opportunity to improve the food stamp program every five years through the Farm Bill. The House passed its version of the bill [in] summer [2007] with an additional $4 billion for food stamps over the next five years. The Senate [passed its version in December 2007].

A Good Public Investment

The three most basic human needs are food, clothing and shelter. It is a national tragedy that in the world's wealthiest nation, more than 25 million Americans, including at least 13 million children, are not able to meet the most fundamental of human needs.

Significantly strengthening the food stamp program would go far toward ending hunger. The General Accounting [now "Accountability"] Office has documented the program's re- markable accuracy. New York has been recognized by the U.S. Department of Agriculture for efficiently managing the pro- gram for three consecutive years. With this level of recognized efficiency and accountability, taxpayers can trust that addi- tional funding and expansion of the food stamp program is a well-managed public investment.

Food stamps are critical to New York, and to our children in particular. The program helps nearly 1.8 million New York- ers, including 724,000 children and almost 300,000 senior citi- zens. It also helps local economies. In 2006, $4.2 billion in

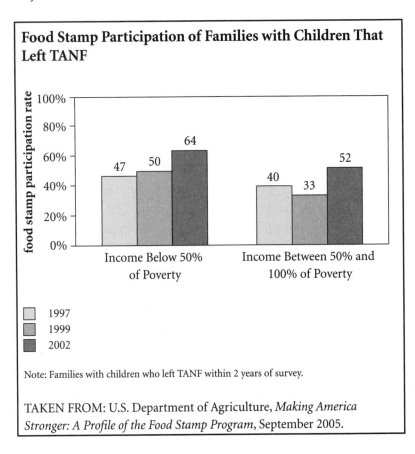

Food Stamp Participation of Families with Children That Left TANF

Note: Families with children who left TANF within 2 years of survey.

TAKEN FROM: U.S. Department of Agriculture, *Making America Stronger: A Profile of the Food Stamp Program*, September 2005.

federal food stamp dollars came into New York's communities. Congress can choose to make meaningful improvements to how food stamps are administered. In July [2007], the House passed a farm bill that would stop the erosion of benefits and restore some of what had been lost. It would provide some relief to the 40,000 elderly and disabled New Yorkers who receive a minimum monthly benefit, which has been stuck at $10 since 1977. . . .

An Increase Is Needed

Benefit levels must be increased. . . . Food stamp benefits for a typical working parent with two children in New York will have dropped in real terms by $24 a month since 1995.

I learned firsthand what life on a food stamp budget was like in May [2007], when I took the "Food Stamp Diet Challenge." I agreed to live on a daily food budget of $1.16 a meal, the amount of the average food stamp benefit in New York. Living on this budget for a week is nothing like experiencing it continuously, but it does offer a glimpse.

Act Now

I was shocked and saddened by this experience. I learned how stressful managing food on a tight budget is. I learned that when I left milk out on the counter by mistake, I had no milk for the rest of the week. I managed to eat an apple a day, but could not afford fresh vegetables. Each breakfast, lunch and dinner that week was exactly the same because I had to buy in bulk as much as possible. I became quite lethargic and irritable. My family noticed a big difference in my mood. It became clear that food stamp benefits do not provide the nutrition that people need to function at their best, whether at home, work or school. My heart ached for the adults and children who experience this every day.

We can, and must, eliminate hunger and food insecurity. It is unacceptable to allow our most vulnerable community members to go without adequate food. . . . Action must be taken now.

Periodical Bibliography

The following articles have been selected to supplement the diverse views presented in this chapter.

Michael Anft	"Grant Makers Shift Focus from Welfare to New Projects to Reduce Poverty," *Chronicle of Philanthropy*, March 8, 2007.
Peter Beresford	"Let's End Divide and Rule," *Community Care*, October 4, 2007.
David Boyle	"Is This How to End Public Service Failure?" *New Statesman*, February 23, 2004.
Matthew Cooper	"The Welfare Merry-Go-Round: Part 2," *Time*, September 22, 2003.
Brian Doherty	"Immigration and the Welfare State," *Reason*, August 2006.
Rodger Doyle	"Welfare Woes," *Scientific American*, May 2006.
Economist	"From Welfare to Workfare," July 29, 2006.
Economist	"Tough Love Works," July 29, 2006.
Steven Greenhouse	"From Work to Welfare? Reversal Feared in City Layoffs," *New York Times*, May 21, 2003.
Charles Karelis	"What Keeps Poor People Poor," *Chronicle of Higher Education*, June 29, 2007.
Susan E. McGregor	"Cash Assistance Is Down, but Incomes Are Stagnant," *Amsterdam (NY) News*, January 12, 2006.
Ellen Reese	"The Causes and Consequences of U.S. Welfare Retrenchment," *Journal of Poverty*, vol. 11, no. 3, 2007.
Techniques: Connecting Education & Careers	"Education and Training Are Critical Tools to Helping Welfare Recipients Achieve Self-Sufficiency," March 2004.

CHAPTER 4

What Are Some Alternatives to the Current Welfare System?

Chapter Preface

In 1995, a year before the enactment of sweeping welfare reform legislation, David Forte, a professor of law at Cleveland State University, noted in an article that the trend in welfare thinking was to throw money at federal and state programs while ignoring the indispensable role of private charities in helping the needy. "This is unfortunate, especially for the poor," Forte wrote. "Private charities typically provide more meaningful assistance to poor families and households because they cater their services to people's specific needs and problems. Many poor families turn first to private sector agencies rather than public agencies when they need emergency services such as shelter and counseling." He advocated tax breaks and other incentives for Americans to help support charities so that these organizations could expand their role in the welfare equation.

Other scholars and pundits, including Howard Husock—a think-tank member represented in the following chapter, have pushed for increasing the outreach of private charities and donor organizations so that government welfare could be reduced or eliminated. Like Forte, Husock contends that private charities are usually sought out by the disadvantaged because they are typically more caring and accommodating than bureaucracies. Some proponents even argue that engendering the caring spirit of public service is a worthwhile goal of placing charitable giving over government handouts. That is, each community would be better served if it learned to take care of all of its members without recourse to state or federal institutions.

Some who support privatization of welfare are not ready to relinquish all responsibilities to charities but are willing to invest private corporations with certain welfare duties. Governor Mitch Daniels of Indiana is noted for enacting a plan in

2006 to turn over the processing of food stamps, Medicaid, and other welfare benefits to a consortium led by business machine giant IBM. Daniels hopes the outsourcing will save Indiana money, but his critics fear that corporate control is no more efficient or compassionate than government bureaucracy. In fact, a similar plan in North Carolina ran afoul of poor management, and the state government had to cancel the corporate contract when clients' Medicaid bills were not paid in a timely manner.

The radical act of transferring welfare responsibilities to private organizations and the less revolutionary move of privatizing the disbursement of welfare are but two examples of how many politicians and interested scholars are contemplating alternatives to the traditional welfare system. In the following chapter, Howard Husock and other commentators debate various proposals to revamp or overturn welfare practices. Though most of these plans remain controversial, the debate reveals that the overriding concern of all involved is the well-being of the poor and a reduction of poverty in America.

| "*Inclusion of everyone in asset-based policy will reduce social inequality and divisions.*"

Low-Income Families Should Be Encouraged to Build Their Own Assets

Michael Sherraden

In the following viewpoint, Michael Sherraden argues that consumer spending among the poor is not a useful indicator of their economic strength. He contends that in order to improve the financial security of the poor, the United States should adopt a widespread plan to build the assets of all Americans. He proposes that the nation create long-term savings programs that would be funded by individual contributions, government welfare, workplace payments, and private donations. These accounts could be started early in a person's life so that the money would be available in later years for housing purchases, education, and business capital. Michael Sherraden is a professor of social development and the director of the Center for Social Development at Washington University in St. Louis.

Michael Sherraden, "From the Social Welfare State to the Social Investment State," *Shelterforce Online*, March/April 2003. Reproduced by permission of the National Housing Institute.

As you read, consider the following questions:

1. What are the three reasons that asset-building would be beneficial for children, in Sherraden's view?
2. Why does Sherraden say that asset-building strategies are not primarily about fighting poverty?
3. In the author's view, what four barriers do low-income persons face in accumulating assets?

The welfare state at the start of the 21st century appears to be in the midst of a transformation. The original consensus was that, if the market economy was sufficiently productive, it could be taxed to support social expenditures. These social expenditures were assumed to be a diversion of capital from production and a drag on economic growth.

Today, the assumed competition between social protection and economic growth is being challenged. There is increasing recognition that social spending for some purposes and/or in some forms can contribute to both economic growth and social development. Reflecting this, the best social policy alternatives will move beyond the idea of consumption-as-well-being [i.e., looking at spending levels as an indicator of people's economic security] toward what [Indian economist] Amartya Sen identifies as capabilities. Building people's assets is one policy pathway to both increase capabilities and eliminate the trade-off between economic growth and social development in the process.

Shaping New Policy

Consistent with this perspective, social policy in the 21st century may have three major goals:

Social protection goals. To buffer hardship and promote social stability has been the primary—almost exclusive—theme of 20th century welfare states. The focus is on standard of living coverage, and adequacy and minimum protections at the bottom. This is social welfare defined in terms of income and consumption.

Development goals. Promoting the economic and social development of families and households and their active participation in work, community and civic affairs may become as important as social protection goals.

Macroeconomic goals. Increasingly, social policy will be formulated with macroeconomic considerations in mind, including countercyclical spending [i.e., spending during periods of economic slowdown] fiscal stability, savings and investment, and economic growth.

In other words, social policy appears likely to move beyond consumption support, aiming for greater social and economic development of households, communities, and the society and economy as a whole. An active social policy that promotes engagement is better suited to the post-industrial economy.

Benefits of Asset-Building

Asset-based policy is a major social policy transformation occurring in many countries, but as yet little recognized. Asset holding has many positive effects for individuals and families, including greater long-term thinking and planning for the future, increased participation in the community and investments in self, financial instruments and enterprise for greater returns.

Although sometimes called "privatized," the state is a major participant in the new asset-based policy. Much of the policy is delivered via accounts such as 401(k) [retirement plan], college savings plans and the like. The state is leading the way by defining these policies, regulating them and providing tax benefits as subsidies for asset accumulation. This is very likely a historic transition toward asset accounts as a main social policy instrument—a transition from Social Welfare State to Social Investment State.

But the poor, who do not qualify for the tax benefits, are usually left behind. Asset-based tax benefits are extraordinarily regressive. The well-off get almost all of the benefits. Thus, the state is, perhaps unwittingly, becoming part of the structure of asset inequality. It is important to note that no universal, progressive, asset-based policy exists anywhere today.

Experimentation in the United States

The idea of a progressive asset-based policy in the form of Individual Development Accounts (IDAs) was introduced more than a decade ago and has become more common with each passing year. IDAs are matched savings for particular purposes, usually homeownership, education or small business capitalization. [The IDAs are implemented by community organizations and funded by private and public sources.] IDAs were not intended to be small community projects, but rather a universal policy system. We are taking steps in this direction.

At the Center for Social Development, we have been studying the American Dream Demonstration, an IDA demonstration implemented by the Corporation for Enterprise Development and supported by 11 foundations, with the Ford Foundation and Charles Stewart Mott Foundation playing leading roles. We are learning that even the very poor can save when there are a structure and incentives to do so. It is noteworthy that people of very low incomes (under 50 percent of the poverty line), controlling for other factors, save as successfully as people with greater incomes (up to 200 percent of the poverty line). In other words, those with very low incomes save at a higher rate than high-income individuals.

Vision and leadership will be required to include all of the poor in asset accumulation policies and to make asset accumulation lifelong. Inclusion of everyone in asset-based policy will reduce social inequality and divisions and increase economic activity and growth. New thinking and new calculations on the part of government will be required. In the Social Investment State, there is not necessarily a trade-off between redistribution and growth. Promoting and subsidizing asset holding by the poor can contribute to growth in the long term.

Focus on Children

Asset holding may make the most sense in the case of children for several reasons. First, asset building is a long-term process. Starting early will result in greater accumulations. Second, asset holding probably changes outlook and attitudes in positive ways. And we know that it is far easier and more effective to change outlook and attitudes earlier in life rather than later. Third, the whole family can be engaged around asset-based policy for children.

Among many possible asset-based policy options, the proposed Child Trust Fund of Prime Minister Tony Blair in the United Kingdom, which would be universal and progressive, offers the greatest opportunity for long-term transition toward an inclusive asset-based policy. IDA research results in the United States helped influence the Blair proposal. Over time, a Child Trust Fund could develop into a system of life-long accounts for the entire population.

Policies similar to the Child Trust Fund have been proposed in the United States for several years, and they are gradually gaining prominence and support within both major political parties. An important demonstration of children and youth accounts is being planned by the Corporation for Enterprise Development. If the United Kingdom were to move ahead with a Child Trust Fund, it could become the final push that creates a similar policy across the Atlantic and could ultimately influence policy in many nations.

Eventually, we may be asking: why not a child saving account for every child on the planet? Although this seems far

Individual Development Accounts

Individual Development Accounts (IDAs) form the primary vehicle for Asset Building in the United States. They are matched savings accounts held with financial institutions, usually banks and credit unions. The sponsors normally manage the private programmes, and the states tend to work with the same or similar groups. Thus, so far at least ... the local, community-based character of service delivery has been preserved, indeed held central in programme administration. Match rates vary, with 1:1 and 2:1 the most common. Saving periods normally extend three years. The standard uses of the matched funds are home ownership, education or training and starting small businesses. A few programmes allow one or more broader uses, such as retirement income, home repair and purchase of a computer or an automobile. Programmes tend to focus on the working poor as clients. To make sure that clients manage their limited finances well, attendance at training sessions in financial management and economic literacy is usually mandatory as a condition of participation, and programme workers maintain close personal contact with clients to provide counseling and encouragement.

Organisation for Economic Co-operation and Development, 2003.

out of reach today, information technology may one day make this possible. Not only technological but political challenges would be great, but it may be worth the effort. What better way to invest in economic and social development?

Asset-Building Policy Principles

Any asset-based policy system should complement, not replace, existing income-based policies. A mature asset-based policy should be shaped by four core principles: inclusiveness, progressivity, coherence and development.

Perhaps the most important issue is inclusion. The goal should be an asset-based policy that is large scale and fully inclusive, with progressive funding, so that everyone participates and has resources for life investments and social protections. The policy could include everyone beginning at birth, as with the UK Child Trust Fund, which would be the most sensible and desirable approach.

In asset-based policy, solidarity should come up front with progressive deposits into accounts of the poor. Current asset-based policy in every country in the world is regressive. The minimum standard should be equal subsidies in currency units (not percent of income) for everyone. For example, whatever tax benefits a wealthy person receives on a pension account should be equaled by direct deposits into the account of a poor person. A better, but more radical, principle would be progressive deposits in currency units—greater subsidies for the poor, as proposed for the UK Child Trust Fund.

Asset-based policy is not primarily about problem amelioration or fighting poverty. It is about enabling individuals and families to be in control of their lives, develop capabilities, and contribute to society and the economy. While this will involve tackling poverty, we should remember that the central goal of asset-based policies is development in a broader context. It is about building the capacity of people with low incomes and allowing them to seek opportunities.

Design Principles

There are signs that policy makers around the world are beginning to realize the importance of developing inclusive asset-building policies. A number of design issues should be borne in mind if this thinking is to lead to successful policy implementation.

Extension. It is easier to extend current policy than to create new policy. In the United States this could include democratization of existing pension products, such as IRAs [individual retirement accounts] and 401(k)s for all workers. Policy extension can occur in other forms as well. In nations with child allowances, including all of Western Europe, a universal children's savings account could be viewed as an extension of the allowance.

Institutional framework. Institutional arrangements largely determine who accumulates assets. Low-income persons face four barriers: insufficient income tax liability to take advantage of tax benefits for savings and asset accumulation; weak or no attachments to the formal labor market, where most structured asset accumulation occurs; asset limits in public assistance programs, which are disincentives to save; and a greater likelihood of not being part of the financial mainstream, or being "unbanked" [i.e., not having a bank account], which makes asset accumulation nearly impossible. Asset-based welfare should extend institutional arrangements for asset accumulation to low-income, low-wealth persons.

Infrastructure. In "The Universal Piggy Bank: Designing and Implementing A System of Savings Accounts for Children," Fred Goldberg and Jodi Cohen have argued that if the government set up accounts for everyone beginning at birth and did nothing else, this would be a major step forward. Goldberg refers to this as "putting the plumbing in place." If the plumbing (universal asset accounts) were in place for everyone, resource flows, both public and private, would be facilitated.

Simplicity and cost control. The key to cost control is simplicity and will likely mean a policy instrument with centralized administration and one or only a few investment options. One alternative is that individuals own shares of an asset pool invested by government (or an agent of government). A second alternative is limited individual investment choices from low-cost mutual fund (unit trust) companies. This simple, low-cost system can be complemented by financial education and other supports at the community level where necessary, but such costly features should not be part of the basic policy.

Pathway to scale. It may not always be possible to reach everyone at the outset or fully fund a large-scale policy. In these circumstances it may be necessary to start small but with a policy design that can be expanded over time. To end up with a large, low-cost program, it is not a good idea to begin with a small, high-cost program. This is what has occurred with IDAs in the United States. We are now in the process of designing low-cost policy models that will work on a larger scale.

A Viable Future

It is enormously challenging to create a universal, progressive asset-based policy. The odds against success are great. However, it is useful to recall that early in the 20th century the odds against creating a universal, progressive social insurance policy were also great. Yet by century's end social insurance had become, in a fiscal sense, the central characteristic of modern states.

By the end of the 21st century the social policy landscape will again look very different. Asset-based policy is likely to continue growing, possibly replacing social insurance as the dominant form of policy in advanced economies. Various types of asset accounts may be integrated into a single, multi-purpose policy system. Everyone might have an account from birth with funds accumulated for education, homeownership, life and health insurance, some aspects of medical care and retirement. In the United States, it seems likely that existing asset accounts—IRAs, Medical Savings Accounts, 401(k)s, Individual Training Accounts, Educational Savings Accounts, IDAs and so on—will merge into one system. It is important to consider how this evolving system can include unbanked persons and provide them with equivalent incentives to participate through direct deposits and refundable tax credits.

Accounts will also likely be portable, potentially across national boundaries. For example, one can imagine a policy system that is perfectly integrated in the European Community and perhaps in North America. The latter would be the social policy equivalent of NAFTA [North American Free Trade Agreement]. Indeed, with the rapid expansion of information technology, one can imagine a worldwide system of asset accounts that is fully portable anywhere on the planet.

Inclusion will be the major challenge. If we stay on the present course, the poor will continue to be excluded from asset accumulation and will not fully participate in the emerging system. If inclusion is to be achieved, it will rest on the widespread recognition that asset building is a sensible public investment because it increases the capabilities, engagement and productivity of the people.

"*Without doubt the poor need assets,
... but we can neither save nor incentivize our way out of poverty.*"

Current Asset-Building Strategies Are Ineffective

Jared Bernstein

*Jared Bernstein is the director of the Living Standards program
at the Economic Policy Institute, an economic policy think tank.
He has previously served as chief economist for the U.S. Department of Labor. In the following viewpoint, Bernstein argues that
Individual Development Accounts (IDAs)—the most common
form of asset-building program in the United States—are not a
successful strategy to help low-income Americans save for education, home building, or other life priorities. Bernstein contends
that most poor workers cannot afford to save enough to make
such accounts yield significant profits. Unless such savings programs were expanded to a much larger scale, Bernstein believes
that debates over the value of IDAs merely distract policy makers
from raising the minimum wage or bolstering other practical
programs to help the poor.*

As you read, consider the following questions:

1. What does Bernstein claim is the common liberal objection to IDAs?
2. According to the author, what are the two obstacles that "stand between the working poor and their fair slice of the economic pie"?
3. Why do supporters of grand-scale asset-building policies resurrect the Homestead Act and the GI Bill in support of their argument, as Bernstein relates?

The problem of poverty in America looms large even in the best of times. The most recent economic boom [ca. 2002] got the share of those officially deemed poor down to 11.7 percent, or about 33 million persons, but poverty rates are much higher for economically vulnerable groups such as single mothers, African Americans and Hispanics. Advocates of savings incentives and other asset-building programs for the poor convincingly and passionately make the case that while low incomes are the proximate cause of poverty at any point in time, the inability to accumulate wealth is what keeps people and their families stuck in poverty for generations. As Ray Boshara, who directs the asset-development program at the New America Foundation, wrote in a [September 2002] *New York Times* op-ed, "Lack of income means you don't get by; lack of assets means you don't get ahead." Income supports are a necessary palliative; asset building could be curative.

Poor Cannot Afford to Save

The asset-building idea that has gone farthest politically and has the greatest bipartisan support is the Individual Development Account (IDA), a subsidized savings account. IDA demonstration projects currently going on around the country, funded by a 1998 federal pilot program and by nonprofit groups, work like this: Low-income persons make deposits to an IDA and their withdrawals—so long as they are for approved expenditures, such as education, housing or an independent business—are matched at a multiple, typically 2-to-1 or 3-to-1. The amount of dollars matched is capped to control program costs. The approach combines a savings incentive with a form of income distribution, in the hope of encouraging the poor to acquire the financial habits of the middle class. What could be wrong with that?

A common objection from liberals is that IDAs are fine as far as they go, but the poor can't save enough to make much difference, even with the incentive of generous matches. This, by itself, wouldn't be so bad, critics say, but the effort that think tanks, advocates and policymakers are putting into asset development is taking energy and resources away from other activities that could make a difference.

Research on IDAs does suggest, not surprisingly, that most of the poor are hard pressed to save much. Michael Sherraden, the grand old man of asset-building policies for the poor, and his colleagues recently completed what they call "the first systematic study" of IDAs. They found that low-income participants were only able to put away a net value of about $20 per month on average, with a median of about $10, leading to annual average accumulations—including the average 2-to-1 match—of around $700. It's hard to imagine that this level of saving could generate the kinds of investments that can change the economic trajectory of a poor family.

Shifting Focus Away

What's more, it is a select group of low-income persons who have volunteered to participate in the current demonstration programs, so the study results probably represent the upper end of what most low-income persons likely can save. As Sherraden et al. report, relative to all low-income families, the participants studied were "better educated, more likely to be employed and more likely to have a bank account." Sherraden also found that two-thirds of the participants made un-

Saving Is Not the Problem

IDAs' claims to encourage thrift, work and self-reliance are responsive. One might infer that lack of old-fashioned virtues is the root of economic distress. But if you believe that poverty results not from lack of thrift, but from employers' power to squeeze wages and to defund social insurance . . . then irresponsible personal behavior is not the problem. IDAs do not address fundamental class questions of inequality and power.

As an aside, there is something a little absurd about the implication that the poor's problems are founded on inadequate saving. The federal government is spending much more than it takes in, and the United States is buying much more from other countries than it sells.

Max B. Sawicky, TomPaine.com, February 7, 2005.

matched withdrawals from their IDAs. That's strong evidence of how cash-strapped these poor savers are: They sacrificed $2 later because they needed $1 now (though advocates correctly point out that some of these folks were just using the program to get low-cost banking services).

On the other hand, for the minority (about one-third) of participants who made approved, and thus matched, withdrawals, the average value of their savings plus the match was about $2,500. And a small number of these participants were able to purchase homes or micro-enterprises, or pay for higher education. Presumably these people didn't finance their acquisitions on the basis of the IDA alone, but it surely helped.

So while the poor can't save much, they can save a little (and some more than a little), and the match is clearly redistributive, just like the income-based programs that progressives widely support. Advocates of asset-building programs stress other positive attributes, too. In the demonstration programs, some families put their Earned Income Tax Credit refund in an IDA and got a double-shot of redistribution, as well as a nest egg.

As a matter of practical politics, IDAs have captured the support of Republican legislators hostile to other strategies of income redistribution. Archconservative Sen. Rick Santorum (R-Penn.), for example, is one of the sponsors of a bipartisan IDA bill in the [108th] Congress, which proposes to spend $500 million to create 300,000 IDAs. Does anyone seriously think that, absent IDAs, he'd be suggesting we use those resources to strengthen, say, labor law enforcement?

Some of the skepticism among liberals reflects worries about the individualistic political consciousness embedded in this approach. And indeed, Richard Nadler of the American Shareholders Association, in an article for the Cato Institute (which supports IDAs), predicts that new asset holders will "internalize their new role as capitalists." There's also the legitimate concern that too much emphasis on incentivizing saving distracts us from the structural causes of poverty.

The Poor Lack Power

For the most part, what holds back the poor is neither their personal desire to save (or not to save) nor the unfair tilt in the tax code that creates lucrative savings vehicles for the wealthy. What stands between the working poor and their fair slice of the economic pie is their lack of political power in the policy arena and lack of bargaining power in the labor market. The latter is particularly germane in the era of welfare reform, as the working poor get stuck in low-end jobs without union representation, receiving not even a living wage, much less a fair one. When unemployment was low for a few years in the late 1990s, employers had to jack up wages and even low-wage workers were able to claim a share of the national prosperity, but that was an anomalous period in the context of the last three decades [i.e., since the 1980s], and those days are behind us.

Low-wage workers [in 2003] are subject more than ever to the vicissitudes of the marketplace, their economic opportunities dictated by a Congress that consistently fails to represent their interests. As noted, these politicians, even the conservative ones, may vote to extend them a matched savings plan, allow them to keep a few more assets and still get food stamps, or, like President [George W.] Bush, favor increasing the size limits on IRAs [individual retirement accounts] (as if that were constraining the poor's ability to save). But when it comes to spending real money, if the politicians redistribute at all, they do so in the wrong direction.

IDAs, at least in their current incarnation, don't do much to challenge this status quo. (Though, in fairness, neither do food stamps nor even the Earned Income Tax Credit.) Each of these programs does redistribute some resources to the poor, and that's helpful. But they fail to shift the power dynamics in such a way as to alter the primary distribution of income, to ensure that the fruits of economic growth are fairly shared with those who create them.

IDAs Are Too Insignificant

After looking closely at the lay of the land, I find it hard to make a connection between the goals sought by champions of asset broadening and their horse in the race, IDAs. The real problem, it seems to me, is not the concept of IDAs, which is sound enough, but their possible magnitude in the present political climate.

For asset-building policies to have the transformational impact that their supporters desire, they need to be much bigger and bolder. This is widely realized by those in the movement, who frequently talk about "going to scale."

In fact, when they reminisce about great asset-broadening policies of the past, advocates invariably invoke the Homestead Act and the GI Bill. These were, of course, large and universal programs that didn't nibble at the edges of redistribution; they aggressively sought to remove class barriers and create real equality of opportunity. If we want low-income persons to acquire a meaningful asset—to own a home or a business—we probably have to go well beyond even generous IDAs.

Ray Boshara has a big idea in this spirit. He argues that for $24 billion per year, we could endow every child with a $6,000 savings account, which would grow over time. The savings could be spent only to acquire specified assets such as a home or higher education. The universality of this scheme is a strong political selling point. And while every child would get an account, it would mean more to the poor. However, the program could be made more progressive by raising the amount for low-income children and adding a phase-out at high-income ranges.

Such policies needn't pose an either/or choice for liberals. There's nothing stopping us from fighting for them while pushing for better income supports as well as programs that lift the bargaining power of the least well-off. And when all is said and done, of course, it's hard to imagine anything transformative occurring in any realm of social policy absent a major shift of political power to the left.

Without doubt the poor need assets, and policies that help the poor accumulate them deserve support. But we can neither save nor incentivize our way out of poverty. We still need a better income-based safety net, higher minimum wages, lower unemployment, fairer tax policies, more refundable tax credits, more unions, better protections against discrimination and so on. And we must be mindful that the growing gulf between classes in our political economy translates into highly skewed power relations, a reality that explains why even promising approaches such as IDAs are kept at token levels rather than the scale of the GI Bill.

> *"[Welfare recipients enrolled in microenterprise programs] experienced strong growth in income and employment, and their reliance on . . . cash assistance was greatly reduced."*

Self-Employment Can Build Self-Sufficiency Among Welfare Recipients

Joyce A. Klein, Ilgar Alisultanov, and Amy Kays Blair

The following viewpoint was written by Joyce A. Klein, Ilgar Alisultanov, and Amy Kays Blair. All three are staff members of the Aspen Institute Economic Opportunities Program, which advances strategies that connect the poor and underemployed to the mainstream economy. In the following viewpoint, the authors discuss the results of an ongoing study of welfare recipients who were enrolled in programs that teach the basics of microenterprise (small business startups that would lead to self-employment). Klein and her colleagues conclude that those partaking of microenterprise opportunities were likely to earn steady incomes, acquire more assets, and leave welfare rolls (or at least

Joyce A. Klein, Ilgar Alisultanov, and Amy Kays Blair, "Microenterprise as a Welfare to Work Strategy: Two-Year Findings," Queenstown, MD: Aspen Institute, November 2003. http://fieldus.org. Copyright © 2003 by the Economic Opportunities Program of the Aspen Institute. All rights reserved. Reproduced by permission.

become less dependent on welfare services). The authors suggest, therefore, that funding programs that teach microenterprise skills might be one path for the poor to achieve some degree of self-sufficiency.

As you read, consider the following questions:

1. What is income patching, as Klein and her colleagues define it?
2. According to the authors, by how much had the median income of households participating in the microenterprise program grown between the onset of the program and the Wave 3 interviews two years later?
3. As the authors relate, what percentage of Wave 3 respondents said their independent businesses could grow if they had better child care?

The federal welfare reform legislation of 1996 ushered in a new era of welfare policy: one that combined new work requirements with the idea of time-limited benefits. Seeking to meet the conditions of the federal law, state and local administrators have focused on how to enable recipients to secure private-sector wage employment. For those who may not be able to obtain such employment, there has been talk of public jobs or community services programs. But, relatively little attention has been paid to another form of work for welfare recipients: self-employment.

While self-employment is not a work option that makes sense for most recipients of Temporary Assistance for Needy Families (TANF), there are reasons to believe that it should be part of an economic self-sufficiency strategy for some. Data from the National Survey of America's Families found that seven percent of the TANF leavers it sampled in 1997 were self-employed. This is similar to the national rate of self-employment, which was 8.1 percent in 1997. It is also higher than the self-employment rate among women, which was 6.6

percent in 1997. In rural areas, self-employment is an even more important source of employment—in 2002, 10.4 percent of workers in nonmetropolitan counties were self-employed, compared to 7.2 percent nationwide. And, in some rural areas, the role of self-employment is even more pronounced. For example, a recent study by the Center for Rural Affairs found that nonfarm proprietors constituted 22 percent of employment in rural farm counties throughout the Great Plains states.

Furthermore, individuals at the margins of the workforce have always engaged in self-employment—whether formal or informal—either as a substitute for or a supplement to traditional wage employment. Studies have also found that women on welfare often use self-employment as a means to supplement their wage earnings. And, while there has been little research on the scope of the underground economy on the national level, one study conducted in 1983 estimated that 27.1 percent of adult men and 13.5 percent of adult women were engaged in the informal economy.

Why Consider Self-Employment

Another reason to consider self-employment as a work strategy for welfare recipients is that there are reasons to believe that it may be the best work strategy for some TANF recipients. Studies of self-employment have shown that women with children are significantly more likely to choose self-employment than those without. Their motivation is to find a way to effectively balance their work and family responsibilities—even if this means earning less money. Research has also found that individuals with disabilities are 1.5 times more likely to engage in self-employment. As many in the TANF population face clear barriers to work due to their need to tend to child-care responsibilities, or as they seek to deal with recurring health issues, it makes sense to consider self-employment as a solution.

Recognizing the importance of the self-employment option for some individuals, microenterprise programs in the United States have been helping welfare recipients to start and expand self-employment ventures for more than two decades. In some cases, they seek to assist individuals who may be engaged in informal economic activity to expand and transform their efforts into a formal business. In other instances, they assist individuals who have developed productive skills through wage employment or as a "hobby" to transform those skills into a business.

Under the previous federal welfare program, Aid to Families with Dependent Children (AFDC), the primary barriers that welfare recipients faced in becoming self-employed lay in the eligibility rules regarding the ownership of assets, and the treatment of business income and expenses in determining household income. With the advent of the TANF program, states had the option to create asset and income rules that were more supportive of self-employment. However, work requirements, time limits and the "work first" approach implemented in many states posed other potential barriers to recipients seeking to pursue self-employment.

The Microenterprise Demonstration

Recognizing the challenges posed by this new federal structure, the Charles Stewart Mott Foundation initiated its Microenterprise Welfare to Work Demonstration and Evaluation in 1998, with the goal of examining whether, and under what circumstances, self-employment could be a route to self-sufficiency for TANF recipients. The initiative provided three-year demonstration funding to 10 microenterprise organizations that provided self-employment services to TANF recipients. In addition, the Foundation provided funding to FIELD, the Microenterprise Fund for Innovation, Effectiveness, Learning and Dissemination, to conduct an evaluation of the demonstration.

The 10 demonstration sites . . . each provided a core set of services to the TANF recipients enrolled in their programs. Each grantee developed a set of outreach efforts targeted specifically at TANF recipients. Interested recipients then went through an assessment process in which they worked with the grantees to determine their readiness to engage in self-employment by examining their business concept, their personal readiness and their entrepreneurial skills or aptitudes. After completing the assessment process [in 2000], individuals who enrolled in the programs received business training and technical assistance geared toward teaching basic business skills and the development of an initial business plan. Technical assistance was also provided to participants as they moved through the initial phases of business start-up and operations. All grantees also had business financing programs; all of them also provided some level of employment assistance to individuals who chose to pursue wage employment in addition to or instead of self-employment. . . .

Participants Increased Their Incomes

[In 2002] two years after enrolling in self-employment programs, study participants showed strong increases in their engagement in work. For those who were working, the resulting increase in earned income led to very substantial increases in household income. As a result, the receipt of TANF assistance decreased dramatically, and the percentage of respondents whose families lived below the poverty line also declined. The changes in household income were strongest among the group of participants who drew income from both wage and self-employment—"earned income patchers"—followed by those who earned income from wage employment only, and then those who earned income solely from self-employment.

Study participants also showed increases in household assets, although these were accompanied by substantial increases in household liabilities. As a result, household net worth for

Results of Aspen Institute Study			
Employment Status of Wave 3 Respondents	Wave 1: Intake n=362	Wave 3: Two years later n=362	Change Wave 1 to Wave 3
Self-employment only	65	90	
	(18%)	(25%)	+7%
Wage employment only	60	114	
	(17%)	(31%)	+14%
Both self-employment and wage employment	19	43	
(employment patchers)	(5%)	(12%)	+7%
Total Employment	**144**	**247**	
	(40%)	**(68%)**	**+28%**
Unemployment	207	114	
	(57%)	(31%)	−26%
Unknown	11	1	
	(3%)	(0%)	N/A
Receiving TANF Cash Assistance	339	92	−247
	(94%)	(25%)	(−69%)

TAKEN FROM: Joyce Klein, Ilgar Alisultanov, and Amig Kays Blair, "Microenterprise as a Welfare to Work Strategy," November 2003.

most participants declined. However, individuals who owned businesses did build positive business net worth.

More than half of the study participants operated a business at some point after enrollment in the microenterprise program; this compares to 21 percent who were operating businesses at the time they entered the programs. The businesses that operated throughout the two-year follow-up period showed strong survival rates and growth in monthly sales and business net worth. Many individuals also chose to move between self- and wage employment.

Employment and Welfare Receipt

Two years after program enrollment, 25 percent of the survey respondents were self-employed; 31 percent had wage jobs; and 12 percent were both working and operating a business. Thus, 37 percent of respondents were engaged in self-employment (either solely or in combination with wage employment); 43 percent were engaged in wage employment (again, either solely or in combination with self-employment); and 68 percent were engaged in one or both forms of employment. This compares to 40 percent of respondents who were working—either in self- or wage employment, or in both—at the time of the baseline survey.

Almost half(47 percent) of participants reported having operated a business at some time during the second year following training; 54 percent of respondents reported they had operated a business at some point since enrolling in the microenterprise program. For the most part, respondents who were working were employed full time: those who worked solely in wage or self-employment worked a median of 40 hours per week, while employment-patchers worked a median of 47 hours per week. TANF receipt continued to decline dramatically among the survey sample. At the time of the Wave 3 interviews, [i.e., the third set of interviews conducted two years after the beginning of the program], 25 percent of respondents reported receiving TANF. This compares to 94 percent at program intake.

Household Incomes Grew

Two years after enrolling in the microenterprise programs, the median household income of study participants had grown from $10,114 to $18,952, an increase of 87 percent. As a result, the percentage of respondents living above the poverty line increased: at baseline, 20 percent of respondents had incomes above the poverty line; this increased to 56 percent at the time of the two-year follow-up. Individuals who drew income from a business in tandem with income from a wage job had the highest household income in the sample, followed by those with income solely from a wage job, and those who earned income solely from self-employment. These findings are consistent with other studies of self-employed individuals. Generally, women who are solely self-employed in unincorporated businesses have lower earnings than those who work in wage employment. However, evidence from various studies indicates that individuals who patch wage and self-employment have incomes equal to or greater than those who engage solely in wage employment.

Growth in household income was driven in large part by substantial growth in the personal earnings of respondents, which grew from a median of $355 at the time of enrollment to $7,389 two years later. As a result, the contribution of personal earnings grew from 23 percent to 46 percent of average household income. Increases in earnings and household income led to a resulting decline in the importance of TANF and other forms of public assistance: TANF assistance dropped from 30 percent to 7 percent of household income over the two-year period, while the contribution of food stamps dropped from 19 percent to 6 percent.

Assets, Liabilities, and Net Worth

Over time, survey participants experienced substantial percentage increases in the median value of their household assets, from $425 to $1500. The percent of respondents owning various types of assets grew, in some cases quite markedly. Interestingly, however, growth in the level of liabilities incurred by respondents outpaced the substantial growth in assets. As a result, median net worth declined from $0 to -$680. While much of the growth in liabilities was due to increases in mortgages, and education and vehicle loans—which are arguably used to purchase assets that can result in greater income and wealth over time—a large portion was also attributable to increases in credit card debt.

Interestingly, the subgroup of respondents with income solely from self-employment showed the strongest growth in both assets and liabilities. This seems to be due in part to the relatively high percentage of these respondents who owned real estate and vehicles. Overall, however, the net worth status of individuals with income solely from self-employment was not greatly different from that of the overall sample; they, too, saw net worth decline over the study period, from $0 to $449.

Business Growth

The types of businesses started by study participants varied widely: from child care to business services to construction. The businesses that were in existence at the time of the Wave 3 study had median monthly sales of $668, and median sales of $6500 in the 12 months prior to the interview. Their median business assets were $3,000; 88 percent had positive business net worth, and the median business net worth was $2,800. . . .

The subset of businesses that were at least two years old at the time of the follow-up interview—those that existed at the time of program enrollment and were still operating two years later—showed somewhat stronger performance. The surviving businesses had median monthly sales of $900, median assets of $4,800, and median net worth of $4,000. . . .

Balancing Work and Child Care

The majority of study participants in the . . . microenterprise study are single parents. At the time of the Wave 3 interviews, 93 percent had a dependent child under age 18 living in the household. Forty percent had at least one pre-school age child, and only 25 percent of the sample was living with a spouse or partner. Forty percent of respondents with children had their children in some form of child care during the year prior to the Wave 3 interview. Interestingly, individuals who were solely self-employed were about half as likely to have a child in child care as those who were solely wage employed or those who patched wage and self-employment. This suggests that some respondents may have chosen self-employment because it enables them to better balance their needs to work and to care for their children. While most respondents with children in care found their child care to be reliable, 44 percent of those with businesses said that their businesses could grow if they had better child care.

Microenterprise and Welfare Policy

Demonstration participants clearly progressed in a number of ways in the two years after enrolling in microenterprise programs. Most notably, they experienced strong growth in income and employment, and their reliance on TANF cash assistance was greatly reduced. Individuals who patched income from both self- and wage employment showed the strongest growth in income, and generally experienced lower levels of unemployment.

For welfare agencies considering supporting self-employment, the findings from the study suggest consideration of several factors. First, it is important to recognize that the employment outcomes experienced by individuals who participated in these microenterprise programs involved wage employment and employment patching, as well as self-employment—and that the program designs anticipated and supported this range of outcomes. Secondly, while study participants clearly increased their rates of business ownership, and while the businesses they operated grew over time, at the time of the two-year follow-up, the level of business draw was not sufficient to support the family's full income needs. Given that those who patched self- and wage employment showed the strongest incomes, policymakers may want to consider supporting income patching as a strategy for helping TANF recipients advance toward self-sufficiency. Such support might include orientation sessions that discuss income patching as an option, access to microenterprise training services structured to meet the needs of individuals engaged in wage employment, and access to child care assistance to support the high number of hours worked by income patchers. Finally, welfare agencies may want to look to create policies governing the treatment of business income and assets that allow individuals to reinvest business revenues, as well as to continue to receive some income support as they work to grow their businesses to the point at which they can become a larger source of income support.

> *"Even if [microenterprise development programs] reach very poor clients the programs will not significantly alleviate poverty in the new economy."*

Self-Employment Strategies Are Ineffective for Welfare Recipients

Nancy Jurik

Microenterprise development programs (MDPs) are credited with great success in alleviating poverty in developing countries, helping people to harness their own skills and hard work at small business startups that can lead to self-employment. In the following viewpoint, Nancy Jurik, a sociologist and professor in the School of Justice & Social Inquiry at Arizona State University, questions whether such programs can be equally successful in the United States. In the author's view, although MDPs are touted as market-driven solutions for poverty when government support is in decline, these programs actually do not adequately address the barriers faced by disadvantaged entrepreneurs in

Nancy Jurik, "Introduction," *Bootstrap Dreams: U.S. Microenterprise Development in an Era of Welfare Reform*, Ithaca, NY: ILR Press, an imprint of Cornell University Press, 2005. Copyright © 2005 by Cornell University. All rights reserved. Used by permission of the publisher, Cornell University Press.

today's economy. In addition, Jurik argues, they distract lawmakers and social service providers from addressing the root causes of poverty.

As you read, consider the following questions:

1. What are the three trends listed by Jurik that, in her view, combine to produce the "new economy"?
2. According to the author, why are many MDPs praised by feminists and nonfeminists alike?
3. According to the studies reported by Jurik in this viewpoint, what fraction of MDP clients are actually poor?

The explosion of self-employment programs seems rather abrupt, both in northern hemisphere countries such as the United States that have typically relied on an array of government safety net and job development programs and in southern hemisphere nations that have been dominated by top-down, large-scale modernization planning and assistance. This widespread popularity of MDPs [microenterprise development programs] is integrally linked to global economic restructuring trends and the accompanying neoliberal social policies that justify them.

Compensating for Holes in the Safety Net

[Since the 1970s], policymakers have grown pessimistic about the ability of governments and large businesses to produce sufficient numbers of jobs with livable wages for their citizenry. Several trends, including deindustrialization in northern hemisphere nations, the growth of high-technology industries and jobs, and the increasing globalization of production and consumption, have combined to produce a phenomenon that many refer to as the new economy. Although some have applauded the opportunities associated with the new economy, researchers have also documented its contribution to a growing sense of insecurity for a large percentage (if not the majority) of individuals in the world today. The intensifying worldwide competition for jobs has greatly increased workplace and economic insecurity for most citizens. Technological developments and global competition among firms has encouraged the reorganization of production jobs and new national and international divisions of labor. Many formerly unionized, good-paying industrial jobs with benefits that were taken for granted in northern [i.e., developed] nations have been relocated to the south [i.e., developing nations] in an effort to reduce wages and other production costs. Remaining northern jobs have been reorganized and either downsized or redefined as contingent work: they have become subcontracted, part-time, and temporary positions. The growth of low-paid service-sector jobs has outpaced the development of higher-paying knowledge-intensive positions. Contingent work opportunities along with the underemployment associated with them have stimulated informal economic and self-employment activities. Employment security has declined and individuals must often piece together multiple jobs to support themselves and their families. . . .

Even wealthy northern nations are under pressure to cut social investment and safety net programs and to reduce industrial protections and regulations. In countries such as the United States, this has meant large cuts in welfare, educational, and health-care spending and increasing rates of underemployment, poverty, and child-care problems. In 1996, President Bill Clinton signed the Personal Work and Responsibility Act, which is credited with ending welfare as we knew it. This law ended the federal entitlement to assistance that dated to the Social Security Act of 1935, instituted a program that limited the duration of welfare benefits, and incorporated mandatory work requirements even for mothers with small children.

With the decline of safety net programs, policymakers stressed an increased reliance on informal economic sectors and small businesses to provide jobs and increase the economic well-being of the citizenry. Microenterprise development has been offered as one avenue for incorporating the poor and economically marginalized into the market economy. MDPs are said to promote self-sufficiency and economic development in impoverished communities. These virtues are contrasted with welfare and other safety net programs that are derided for promoting dependency and lowered self-esteem among the poor.

How MDPs Serve Political Agendas

MDPs blend well with neoliberal agendas advocating the privatization of government functions. Traditionally, the term *privatization* refers to the sale of industries formerly owned and operated by government to private-sector firms and the subcontracting of services formerly performed by government to privately owned firms and nonprofits. Because many MDPs are operated by nongovernmental, nonprofit, and, increasingly, even for-profit groups, they are praised for relying on market-based principles and eschewing heavy government involvement.

Recently, privatization trends have escalated, and they now include proposals for the reconceptualization of government services. Jill Quadagno a sociologist, has critically analyzed a trend toward what she calls the "capital investment welfare state," whereby public benefits are being restructured so that they better reflect the principles of the marketplace. This restructured state shifts collective responsibility for its citizens' well-being onto individuals through personal investing, savings, and asset accumulation programs. Calling for the alleviation of poverty through self-employment assistance rather than through more traditional welfare and safety net programs is quite consistent with the growing capital-investment welfare state described by Quadagno.

The market-based strategy for dealing with poverty has enhanced their popularity, but the widespread appeal of MDPs draws on fundamental values of social welfare that cross the political spectrum. For economic conservatives on the political right, MDPs invoke sentiments of *individualism*, appealing to long-held values of faith in free enterprise, the entrepreneurial spirit, self-sufficiency, and pulling oneself up by one's bootstraps. MDPs offer to mediate the negative effects of global capitalism without large-scale permanent government safety net programs (e.g., welfare).

Contemporary liberals and communitarians admire MDPs for their *integrative* functions. They offer disadvantaged people opportunities to participate more fully in the global economy and therein to be empowered as individuals. To political populists, microlending promotes a greening of capitalism by fostering a vision of small-scale entrepreneurs to challenge or at least balance corporate domination. Because many MDPs target women, most of whom work in homebased businesses, these programs are praised by feminists and nonfeminist alike for helping mothers to combine paid work with child-care responsibilities.

For those more left of center, MDPs offers a hope of community mobilization or *collective empowerment*. Borrower groups and other support networks are a strategy for bringing the poor and other disadvantaged groups together to share common problems. This sharing and networking may provide them with a heightened awareness and an organizational base from which to collectively confront structural inequalities emanating from global capitalism. In some southern nations, clients actually own and control MDPs, and, as noted, some MDPs grew out of efforts to organize informal sector workers. Local control of MDPs leads proponents to suggest that the programs can help build viable community-controlled non-bureaucratic organizational forms.

A Developing-World Program in the United States

Can microenterprise programs work as well in the United States as in the developing world?. . . Microenterprise for the US poor is more difficult than in the developing world. Microenterprise is a good choice for a few extraordinary poor people, but wage jobs, additional education, and job training are still the most common paths out of poverty.

Two large-scale tests of US microenterprise development programs suggest that impacts may be small. In a randomized experiment, access to microenterprise programs about doubled the rate of movement from unemployment to self-employment, but the absolute increase in the number of people who moved was only about one per 100. Likewise, take-up rates in a nationwide demonstration of microenterprise programs aimed at recipients of public assistance suggest that access would move, at most, about one person per 1,000 from public assistance to microenterprise. It seems that few poor people in the United States will use self-employment to escape working poverty.

In the United States, abundant wage jobs and an effective public safety net decrease the push to self-employment. Most microenterprise programs in the developing world make loans to the poor through groups, but groups in the United States tend to fall apart because of lack of social capital and because individuals with a good credit record can get loans on their own. The two most important constraints on self-employment in the United States are a lack of savings and/or a lack of skills, but microenterprise programs are limited in how they can facilitate savings, and it is difficult and costly to build the human capital required for entrepreneurship.

Mark Schreiner and Gary Woller,
World Development, *September 2003.*

Research on MDP Effectiveness

The research on MDPs identifies both program strengths and weaknesses. Proponents draw on research to praise MDPs as an avenue for alleviating poverty without heavy governmental expenditures; other analysts question whether MDPs can or even should serve the poor. However, conclusions are weakened by methodological difficulties with study designs.

Much research on microenterprise development has focused on programs in southern hemisphere nations. . . . The relatively fewer U.S. studies also report that MDPs promote business growth, create jobs, and increase client incomes, self-esteem, and community involvement. One seven-year study by the U.S. nonprofit Aspen Institute reports that MDPs develop and stabilize businesses, create jobs, and alleviate poverty. Other research reports significant gains in household income, some large enough to move clients out of poverty. "The average change in household income was $8,484—rising from $13,889 to $22,374 over five years." A study of [international nonprofit microfinance organization] ACCION's U.S. programs reports that clients increased their net income by $450 or more per month. Other evaluations report that MDPs move individuals from unemployment and welfare assistance to economic independence.

Despite the many proclamations of MDP achievements, data on their long-term success are neither complete nor unequivocal. Evaluations in the United States and elsewhere are weakened by methodological problems, including a reliance on indirect measures of success (e.g., loan repayment rates), a lack of adequate comparison groups of nonclients, and lack of long-term follow-up. These components are essential in determining how much movement out of poverty occurs, how much the movement is actually due to MDP interventions, and whether the improved situations persist.

MDP Challenges in the United States

Poverty alleviation goals are especially challenging for U.S. programs. Research on pioneering U.S. MDPs suggests that these programs have even more difficulty in reaching poor entrepreneurs than do their southern hemisphere counterparts. A number of studies conclude that only approximately one-third or less of MDP clients are actually poor, and even those served by MDPs are not among the poorest: they rank significantly above national averages for the poor on assets, education, experience, and skills. Critics charge that MDP program success relies on "creaming," wherein clients with the least likelihood of success are either discouraged by staff from continuation or choose to drop out of the program.

Some researchers in the United States and elsewhere suggest that even if MDPs reach very poor clients the programs will not significantly alleviate poverty in the new economy; that is, they argue that although MDPs may offer valuable assistance to poor microentrepreneurs, the resulting very small businesses rarely grow enough to make significant contributions to the economic growth and employment of their regions. The type of business selected is also a key determinant of success. "Traditional lines of business, such as personal services and small-scale retailing, tend to be favored by clients of microenterprise programs, yet these are the least profitable lines of small business." This tendency is especially problematic for the many women MDP clients who are encouraged to start small-scale, traditionally female businesses, [as] such ventures tend to be labor intensive, low profit, and highly unstable. . . .

A Questionable Welfare Alternative

My findings challenge proponent and media images that frame MDPs [as] alternatives to state welfare and job-training programs. Over time, . . . MDPs have found that it is difficult to serve poor and very-low-income clients and still record sufficient program successes to stay in business. Proponent rhetoric about self-help and client motivation also have often distracted from issues of structural disadvantage and reinforced images that poor and low-income people are responsible for their failures.

Given current trends toward a capital-investment welfare state, it is important to understand the contradictions surrounding microenterprise development. Can MDPs really alleviate poverty in the new economy? If they cannot, their claims to do so and associated efforts to use Temporary Assistance for Needy Families (TANF) dollars to fund MDP services only exacerbate and legitimate the state's failure to provide effective programming for the poor. Without deeper analysis, MDP success rhetoric may simply reinforce the hegemony of the market as a solution to all social problems. Understanding the embedded process of microenterprise development can improve MDP practice and framing so as to encourage the recognition of other viable policy alternatives.

> "America is so wealthy that enabling everyone to have a decent standard of living is easy."

Government Grants to All Adults Should Replace Welfare

Charles Murray

In the following viewpoint, Charles Murray insists that the welfare state cannot be maintained because of its ballooning expense. He proposes scrapping welfare and simply returning tax money to Americans in equal shares. These shares could then be invested in stocks that would yield significant returns over a person's lifetime. According to Murray, this plan would not only give everyone—rich and poor—a chance to secure his or her future, but it would also compel Americans to become more personally and socially responsible. Charles Murray is a scholar at the American Enterprise Institute, a conservative think-tank, and the author of In Our Hands: A Plan to Replace the Welfare State, *in which he elaborates on the concepts presented in this viewpoint.*

As you read, consider the following questions:

1. How does Murray's plan tackle the subject of paying for health care?

2. If Murray's plan had been adopted in 2006, in what year would it begin to cost less than the expected price of the current welfare system?

3. In relation to his plan, what does the author mean when he quotes Aristotle's claim that virtue is habit?

This much is certain: The welfare state as we know it cannot survive. No serious student of entitlements thinks that we can let federal spending on Social Security, Medicare and Medicaid rise from its current 9% of gross domestic product [GDP] to the 28% of GDP that it will consume in 2050 if past growth rates continue. The problems facing transfer programs for the poor are less dramatic but, in the long term, no less daunting; the falling value of a strong back and the rising value of brains will eventually create a class society making a mockery of America's ideals unless we come up with something more creative than anything that the current welfare system has to offer.

So major change is inevitable—and Congress seems utterly unwilling to face up to it. Witness the Social Security debate of [2005], a case study in political timidity. Like it or not, we have several years to think before Congress can no longer postpone action. Let's use it to start thinking outside the narrow proposals for benefit cuts and tax increases that will be Congress's path of least resistance.

Collect Taxes, Divide Them, Return Them

The place to start is a blindingly obvious economic reality that no one seems to notice: This country is awash in money. America is so wealthy that enabling everyone to have a decent standard of living is easy. We cannot do it by fiddling with the entitlement and welfare systems—they constitute a Gordian

Knot that cannot be untied. But we can cut the knot. We can scrap the structure of the welfare state.

Instead of sending taxes to Washington, straining them through bureaucracies and converting what remains into a muddle of services, subsidies, in-kind support and cash hedged with restrictions and exceptions, just collect the taxes, divide them up, and send the money back in cash grants to all American adults. Make the grant large enough so that the poor won't be poor, everyone will have enough for a comfortable retirement, and everyone will be able to afford health care. We're rich enough to do it.

Consider retirement. Let's say that we have a 21-year-old man before us who, for whatever reasons, will be unable to accumulate his own retirement fund. We accumulate it for him through a yearly contribution for 45 years until he retires at age 66. We can afford to contribute $2,000 a year and invest it in an index-based stock fund. What is the least he can expect to have when he retires? We are ridiculously conservative, so we first identify the worst compound average growth rate, using constant dollars, for any 45-year period in the history of the stock market (4.3% from 1887—1932). We then assume our 21-year-old will be the unluckiest investor in American history and get just a 4.0% average return. At the end of the 45-year period, he will have about $253,000, with which he could purchase an annuity worth about $20,500 a year.

That's with just a $2,000 annual contribution, equivalent to the Social Security taxes [FICA] the government gets for a person making only $16,129 a year. The government gets more than twice that amount from someone earning the median income, and more than five times that amount from the millions of people who pay the maximum FICA tax. Giving everyone access to a comfortable retirement income is easy for a country as rich as the U.S.—if we don't insist on doing it through the structure of the welfare state.

Health care is more complicated in its details, but not in its logic. We do not wait until our 21-year-old is 65 and then start paying for his health care. Instead, we go to a health insurance company and tell it that we're prepared to start paying a constant premium now for the rest of the 21-year-old's life. Given that kind of offer, the health insurance company can sell us a health care policy that covers the essentials for somewhere around $3,000. It can be so inexpensive for the same reason that life insurance companies can sell generous life insurance cheaply if people buy it when they're young—the insurance company makes a lot of money from the annual payments before eventually having to write the big benefit checks. Providing access to basic medical care for everyone is easy for a country as rich as the U.S.—if we don't insist on doing it through the structure of the welfare state.

The Plan

There are many ways of turning these economic potentials into a working system. The one I have devised—I call it simply "the Plan" for want of a catchier label—makes a $10,000 annual grant to all American citizens who are not incarcerated, beginning at age 21, of which $3,000 a year must be used for health care. Everyone gets a monthly check, deposited electronically to a bank account. If we implemented the Plan tomorrow, it would cost about $355 billion more than the current system. The projected costs of the Plan cross the projected costs of the current system in 2011. By 2020, the Plan would cost about half a trillion dollars less per year than conservative projections of the cost of the current system. By 2028, that difference would be a trillion dollars per year.

Many questions must be asked of a system that substitutes a direct cash grant for the current welfare state. Work disincentives, the comparative risks of market-based solutions versus government guarantees, transition costs, tradeoffs in health coverage, implications for the tax system, and effects on people

Addressing Concerns About Disincentives to Work

[National Review Online editor Kathryn] Lopez: Under your plan, recent college grads would have incentive to bum around, wouldn't they? The government would give them money to do nothing. Get a couple of bums with some guaranteed income and you've got a government disincentive to be productive, don't you?

[Charles] Murray: I think it would be a great boon to the maturity of our new college grads, and save many innocent people from going to law school, if more of them took a few years after college and did something besides heading straight to grad school or throwing themselves into their careers. I'm not worried about this particular form of work disincentive in the Plan. Playing gets old awfully fast. So does living on $10,000 a year.

Lopez: Not to be stuck on stupid here, but I'm watching the French students rioting now [in 2006 over a controversial bill that would allow businesses the freedom to fire workers under the age of 26—without reason—during an initial two-year trial period]. Is there any danger that under your plan we'd be raising a generation of French kids? People who think they are entitled to money for nothing?

Murray: Au contraire. The problem with the French kids isn't that they think they are entitled to money for nothing, but entitled to guaranteed jobs with high salaries and benefits plus all the goodies of the welfare state. People living under the Plan get the $10,000, but they have to make all the decisions about how to run their lives.

Kathryn Jean Lopez,
National Review Online, March 27, 2006.

too young to qualify for the grant all require attention in deciding whether the Plan is feasible and desirable. I think all of the questions have answers, but they are not one-liners; I lay them out in my book [*In our Hands: A Plan to Replace the Welfare State*, 2006].

The Welfare State Drains Life

For now, let me turn to a larger question: Assuming that the technical questions have answers, do we want a system in which the government divests itself of responsibility for the human needs that gave rise to the welfare state in the first place? I think the reasons for answering "yes" go far beyond the Plan's effects on poverty, retirement and health care. Those issues affect comparatively small minorities of the population. The more profound problem facing the world's most advanced societies is how their peoples are to live meaningful lives in an age of plenty and security.

Throughout history until a few decades ago, the meaning of life for almost everyone was linked to the challenge of simple survival. Staying alive required being a contributing part of a community. Staying alive required forming a family and having children to care for you in your old age. The knowledge that sudden death could happen at any moment required attention to spiritual issues. Doing all those things provided deep satisfactions that went beyond survival.

Life in an age of plenty and security requires none of those things. For the great majority of people living in advanced societies, it is easily possible to go through life accompanied by social companions and serial sex partners, having a good time, and dying in old age with no reason to think that one has done anything significant.

If you believe that's all there is—that the purpose of life is to while away the time as pleasantly as possible—then it is reasonable to think that the purpose of government should be to enable people to do so with as little effort as possible. But if you agree with me that to live a human life can have transcendental meaning, then we need to think about how human existence acquires weight and consequence.

For many . . . , the focus of that search for meaning is bound up with vocation—for some, the quest to be rich and famous; for others, the quest to excel in a vocation one loves. But it is an option open only to a lucky minority. For most people—including many older people who in their youths focused on vocation—life acquires meaning through the stuff of life: the elemental events associated with birth, death, growing up, raising children, paying the rent, dealing with adversity, comforting the bereaved, celebrating success, applauding the good and condemning the bad; coping with life as it exists around us in all its richness. The chief defect of the welfare state from this perspective is not that it is ineffectual in making good on its promises (though it is), nor even that it often exacerbates the very problems it is supposed to solve (though it does). The welfare state is pernicious ultimately because it drains too much of the life from life.

Personal Accountability

The Plan returns the stuff of life to all of us in many ways, but chiefly through its effects on the core institutions of family and community. One key to thinking about how the Plan does so is the universality of the grant. What matters is not just that a lone individual has $10,000 a year, but that everyone has $10,000 a year and everyone knows that everyone else has that resource. Strategies that are not open to an individual are open to a couple; strategies that are not open to a couple are open to an extended family or, for that matter, to half a dozen friends who pool resources; strategies not open to a small group are open to a neighborhood. The aggregate shift in resources from government to people under the Plan is massive, and possibilities for dealing with human needs through family and community are multiplied exponentially.

The Plan confers personal accountability whether the recipient wants it or not, producing cascading secondary and tertiary effects. A person who asks for help because he has frittered away his monthly check will find people and organizations who will help (America has a history of producing such people and organizations in abundance), but that help can come with expectations and demands that are hard to make of a person who has no income stream. Or contemplate the effects of a known income stream on the young man who impregnates his girlfriend. The first-order effect is that he cannot evade child support—the judge knows where his bank account is. The second-order effect is to create expectations that formerly didn't exist. I call it the Doolittle Effect, after Alfred Doolittle in "My Fair Lady." Recall why he had to get to the church on time.

The Plan confers responsibility for dealing with human needs on all of us, whether we want it or not. Some will see this as a step backward, thinking that it is better to pay one's taxes, give responsibility to the government and be done with it. I think an alternative outlook is wiser: The Plan does not require us all to become part-time social workers. The nation can afford lots of free riders. But Aristotle was right. Virtue is a habit. Virtue does not flourish in the next generation because we tell our children to be honest, compassionate and generous in the abstract. It flourishes because our children practice honesty, compassion and generosity in the same way that they practice a musical instrument or a sport. That happens best when children grow up in a society in which human needs are not consigned to bureaucracies downtown but are part of life around us, met by people around us.

Give Responsibility Back to the People

Simply put, the Plan gives us back the action. Institutions and individuals alike thrive to the extent that they have important jobs to do and know that the responsibility to do them is on their heads. For decades, the welfare state has said to us, "We'll take care of that." As a result, we have watched some of our sources of life's most important satisfactions lose vitality. At the same time, we have learned how incompetent—how helpless—government is when "taking care of that" means dealing with complex human needs. The solution is not to tinker with the welfare state. The solution is to put responsibility for our lives back in our hands—ours as individuals, ours as families, and ours as communities.

| "It is poor children who, under the [cash
| grant] plan, may seriously suffer."

Grants to Adults Would Put Children at Risk

Dalton Conley

Dalton Conley is a professor and chair of the Sociology Department of New York University. In the following viewpoint, Conley argues that conservative scholar Charles Murray's proposal to eliminate welfare and replace it with cash grants to every adult American would not be a wise policy. Although Conley does not discredit Murray's notion of block grants, he does contend that the plan would leave children of the poor vulnerable because it does not set aside enough money for parents to provide health care for their children. Conley also disagrees with Murray's claim that eliminating welfare bureaucracy will compel people to have a more active civic life because the safety net of welfare will no longer care for the disadvantaged. Conley suggests that the increased wealth that attends modern society makes people less willing to spend time in civic duties. People who are well off under Murray's plan, therefore, will likely spend money, not time, on the less fortunate, Conley maintains.

Dalton Conley, "Charles Murray's New Plan," *Boston Review*, September/October 2006. Reproduced by permission of the author.

As you read, consider the following questions:

1. How does Conley discredit Murray's plan's health-care proposal?

2. In the author's view, why are children in America a public good?

3. How would Conley alter Murray's proposal to make it more equitable?

Charles Murray is the E.F. Hutton [a now-defunct stock brokerage whose popular ad years ago claimed, "When E.F. Hutton speaks, people listen"] of social policy: when he talks, people listen. His 1984 classic *Losing Ground* is the authoritative statement about the perverse incentives and negative effects of welfare. *Losing Ground* immediately became the handbook of the [President Ronald] Reagan revolutionaries and, most importantly, the basis of welfare reform a dozen years later. So when Murray proposes something, we pay attention—even if he declares it to be politically infeasible, as he has his newest policy idea, outlined in his latest book, *In Our Hands: A Plan to Replace the Welfare State*. He is being modest—too modest, since his imprimatur alone makes the idea politically possible.

Murray's new New Deal [the name of President F.D. Roosevelt's 1930s welfare plan] would replace all safety-net programs with a flat $10,000 annual per-person grant. Murray does away with welfare (that is, Temporary Assistance to Needy Families), food stamps, Medicaid and Medicare, and even Social Security. He also dumps agricultural subsidies and other forms of corporate assistance. Instead, every American age 21 and older would receive $10,000 a year, of which $3,000 would have to be spent on health insurance. When a person's income from other sources exceeded $50,000, his or her grant would be cut back to $5,000. But that is the only reduction. In other words, [Microsoft cofounder and multibillionaire] Bill Gates gets his check, too. Murray is offering a truly universal benefit—even more comprehensive than Social Security, which can exclude those who have not spent much time in the formal labor market. His only requirement is that the recipient maintain a bank account.

Resurrecting Old Proposals

A guaranteed minimum income à la social-democratic Sweden? Universal health insurance through mandatory enrollment? This is clearly not your father's American Enterprise Institute [the conservative think tank of which Murray is a member]. What Murray is offering is a variant of the "universal basic income" proposal that has been advanced over the past 20 years by a number of leftist academics, most prominently the Belgian political theorist Philippe van Parijs. (In a similar spirit, but with different mechanics, Bruce Ackerman and Anne Alstott proposed a substantial one-time grant rather than annual income in *The Stakeholder Society* [1999].) This basic-income movement has been holding annual conferences, trying to introduce legislation (the most recent effort was a bill brought to the House by Representative Bob Filner, D-CA) and generally beating the drums—all to little avail, at least in the United States. But all that may change now that Murray is on board.

As the saying goes, if you can't beat 'em, join 'em. Murray claims that he has given up trying to eliminate the welfare state, so instead he is focusing his efforts on reforming it. Though Murray does not mention universal basic income, he does trace his proposal to the "negative income tax" scheme advanced by Milton Friedman, the intellectual dean of the right, in the 1940s. In fact, [former President Richard] Nixon proposed a similar idea—the Family Assistance Plan—in 1972 as a way to co-opt the proposals of the [1972 Democratic presidential candidate George] McGovern campaign. So why are we not like Sweden, with a universal guaranteed income? Because liberal democrats in Congress wanted the allowance to be higher and objected to the work requirements in the Nixon plan. (To be fair, some conservatives opposed it as well.) Instead, we got some experiments with a negative income tax. The results—increased marital dissolution, decreased labor-force participation, and longer spells of unemployment—seemed to prove the Right's case for it. That ended the debate over universal income support for a good 30 years. So now we've come back to the future, so to speak. Charles Murray, who used the negative-income-tax experiments in *Losing Ground* (and, in fact, the current volume) to discredit the welfare state, is now advocating for one. So what should we make of Murray's proposal?

Poor Children Will Suffer

If everyone in the world belonged to a single generation, I would say that "the Plan" (as Murray calls his proposal) sounds wonderful. But we do not live in such a world. We live in a world with children. And it is poor children who, under the plan, may seriously suffer.

Start with what it costs to raise a child. Each mother would receive $583 a month and health insurance from age 21 till death. That takes care of the Medicare issue. But what about her children? I pay about $400 per month in health-insurance premiums for my family, and my employer matches that amount, a total of almost $10,000 a year. So the cost for parents is remarkably higher than the $3,000 Murray has allotted. And remember, without Medicare, the money has to be stretched to cover health expenses in old age. So it couldn't possibly cover children too. Children are the second most expensive group of health-care users.

Another non-trivial detail: In order to get the figure of $3,000, Murray has instituted a $2,500 deductible. This essentially means that families without other resources will be able to see a doctor in a catastrophe but not for routine problems and prevention.

Costs Doom Murray's Plan

It might well be true that, fully phased in, Murray's scheme would allow all Americans to save enough to enjoy a higher income in retirement than they can expect to receive under the present [Social Security] system. But you cannot put today's actual and prospective Social Security recipients, who have not had 45 years to save for retirement under Murray's plan, on a flat annual income of $10,000 and expect to survive—not politically, and perhaps not literally. That is why, as with Social Security privatization (another good idea in principle), very large transition costs would persist for decades. This is not a minor detail, to be brushed away. It is a chief argument against.

Clive Crook,
National Journal, *April 1, 2006.*

And then, of course, there is the issue of high-quality child care: a single parent who goes to work full-time is likely to spend his or her entire grant on child care. Even at three dollars an hour, care for one child will cost $120 per week, or about $500 per month, and if the parent has a low-wage job, his or her marginal tax rate becomes pretty steep even with one child, let alone two.

Janet Currie proposes one possible solution to this dilemma in her new book, *The Invisible Safety Net*: instead of giving cash to adults, bolster in-kind benefits for children, such as CHIP [Children's Health Insurance Program], WIC [Women, Infants and Children], food stamps, and day-care assistance. While we can never completely control intrahousehold allocations—for example, food stamps can be sold for about 60 cents on the dollar on Brooklyn's Atlantic Avenue—such non-cash assistance does have the advantage of reaching out to children instead of offering an unconditional reward to all adults.

Still, I appreciate the arguments that Murray makes regarding the inefficiencies of such programs. Democrats have too long been the party of programs more than the party of people. As my first amendments to Murray's plan, I would eliminate all paternalistic programs for children except two: preschool and children's health insurance.

A Private or Public Good?

Will these generous adjustments create the same old perverse incentives for poor single people to have babies? Certainly the argument could be made that anything that lowers the cost of having children will increase the demand for them. However, we must keep in mind that while children's health-care costs are substantial, they still form but a fraction of the total costs. And whereas income support and tax policy increased the supply of children by providing additional income to parents for the birth of each child, in this scenario the grant does not correlate to the number of children.

This raises a fundamental theoretical question of how a society should view children. Are they a private good, provided by and for the parents who bring them into this world? If so, maybe we should abandon them to their parents on the grounds of efficiency, if not morality. Or are they—as the economist Nancy Folbre argues—a public good? In other words, do couples without children subsidize couples with children? Or does the free ride work the other way around, with the childless out spending their time and money on cocktails and vacations, being supported, over the long run, by those who do the care for and invest in children, the future workers and taxpayers?

There is not a single answer to this question. In subsistence economies, such as those in sub-Saharan Africa, the answer is clear: Children are a private good and a public burden. Population pressures and poverty combine to create a Malthusian [like that described by philosopher Thomas Malthus] steady-state equilibrium where having more children makes individual families better off and the environment and community worse off, with populations that double every 20 to 25 years. Children are clearly private goods in Malawi, since the division of labor occurs within the household and there is no social safety net. Surviving children collect firewood (which becomes a more and more onerous task as increased populations cut down more and more trees), walk miles to gather drinking water, and plant and harvest crops. And, of course, in the absence of any safety net, they are also a parent's insurance against old age. Intergenerational transfers flow from children to parents.

But our society—with or without Murray's plan—is different. With a social safety net and a high division of labor and interdependence across the whole of society—and not just within our clans—children are more realistically seen as a public good. Intergenerational transfers have reversed: now adult children are typically the net recipients rather than the source. In fact, I would argue that this reversal is one of the categorical distinctions between the developing world and the developed world. In a modern society with a pronounced division of labor, children are a public good, and I worry that we are abandoning them with his plan.

All Things Are Not Equal

However, Murray writes that government need not worry about the abandonment of children. In his view, by eliminating government bureaucracy and the safety net, the plan will lead to the reinvigoration of American civic life—whose decline he traces to the advent of the modern welfare state. This view is a tad too optimistic, I am afraid. America is a lot richer than it was in the early 1900s. But it is also different in quite a number of other ways. The political scientist Theda Skocpol has shown us that today we are actually much more likely to join an organization and donate money, but we are less willing to donate our time. This is not a result of the welfare state. It is a result of our time becoming more valuable—the paradox of that increased wealth that Murray celebrates.

Moreover, we must also remember that social policy is not just about mutual aid. It is also about equal opportunity. When we keep this in mind, and simultaneously shift the lens of policy from an income framework to an asset paradigm, matters appear more complicated. In the United States we have a relatively strong norm of equality of opportunity: as long as the rules of the game are the same for everyone, we readily accept differential outcomes. And when we think about social policy from this perspective, it is merely acting as insurance, providing a basic level of survival and dignity to those who end up on the losing end of a fair game.

But when we shift our attention to wealth, as opposed to earnings, we find that parents' net worth is a powerful predictor of children's long-term socioeconomic success. In fact, my analysis in *Being Black, Living in the Red* shows that it is the single most powerful predictor of the next generation's outcomes. In other words, the fancy house, the car, the 401(k) [retirement plan], the securities portfolio—the unequal rewards of one generation—warp the rules of the game for the next.

Altering Murray's Plan

So I propose another amendment to the Murray plan, a version of the proposal for an asset entitlement at birth—similar to [former British prime minister] Tony Blair's Baby Bonds program in Britain, but (like the Ackerman-Alstott plan) with some real financial heft. In my version, we would extend the plan to cover zero-year-olds through a one-time grant. That is, at birth, each child in America would receive a $10,000 payment held in trust in a private account invested in U.S. corporate securities (big business should appreciate this influx of cash to the private equity market). Parents would manage the fund until the child turned 18. After that, the child would manage it, as he or she would a 401(k) account. The key is that neither the parents nor the child could withdraw from the account, except for one of the following three occasions: a college or graduate education, a down payment on a home, and retirement at age 70. The account would be private, but with forced savings. We could even allow people to defer a portion of their Murray grant into this fund with the same favorable tax conditions that professionals in the high-wage sector get for their IRAs [individual retirement accounts] and 401(k)s. Now we are talking about a real "ownership society."

Along the same lines, we would need to extend the $10,000 annual payment to 18-year-olds in order to help pay for college when they need it. There are also important political reasons for lowering the minimum age. Welfare forms part of a political compact of rights and responsibilities between a polity and the state. Citizenship has its duties—such as paying taxes, submitting to military drafts, and serving on juries—and its corresponding benefits—police protection, election of representatives, and social insurance. Unless we are about to raise the age of conscription and jury duty to 21, we should lower the grant age to 18.

Finding the Money

So how could we pay for child care, children's health insurance, and an asset policy? How about eliminating the home-mortgage interest deduction, a policy that encourages consumption and discourages savings? We could also reinstate the estate tax, and tax capital gains and dividend income at the same marginal rate as earnings. If that does not provide enough revenue, there are still more sources: raising the cap on payroll taxes from $92,000 to twice that amount. Still not enough? How about a national value-added tax—something that conservatives have advocated to tip the balance further toward investment from consumption (and which is defensible in a world where state sales-tax receipts have fallen because of e-commerce exemptions). Too regressive for liberals? Offer a standard rebate to those with incomes below $50,000, who presumably spend most of their income on necessities. Still not enough? There's always gasoline taxes, getting out of Iraq, canceling weapons programs, and a number of other money-savers—and with Murray's support on the right flank, anything is possible.

| "The stars are aligned for nongovernmental organizations to play a much larger role in assisting those in need."

Welfare Should Be Privatized

Howard Husock

Howard Husock is the vice president of programs at the Manhattan Institute, a conservative economic think tank based in New York. He is also a writer who focuses on housing and other urban policy issues. In the following viewpoint, Husock argues that the government should relinquish its role as welfare provider and turn the responsibility over to private charities. This would correct government mishandling and end the drain on national finances, he asserts. Husock also maintains that philanthropic agencies are better suited to the task of aiding the disadvantaged because they have growing monetary resources, are commonly staffed with caring individuals, and have experience in addressing specific needs.

As you read, consider the following questions:

1. As Husock writes, according to a federal review of state child welfare agencies, how many were found to have fully complied with federal standards?

2. According to the author, what is the trendy term for someone who establishes an assistance program for those in need?

3. Why are public social service agencies difficult to hold accountable or discipline for poor performance, in Husock's view?

No matter whose priorities prevail in [the 2006] budget debate, it is a certainty that the federal government will continue to devote billions to activities known as "social services." These include support for everything from foster care to drug abuse prevention; indeed, the Administration for Children and Families alone supports no less than 60 such programs at an annual cost of nearly $13 billion, in addition to the cash welfare payments it handles. Billions more are spent on such purposes by state and local governments, often through contracts with private "providers." Robust public debate has developed as to whether other parts of the New Deal [the nation's first welfare program, begun in the 1930s] legacy still make sense, but the central role of government in providing or paying for social services appears settled—with the only question being how best to achieve efficiency and effectiveness.

But should this role be considered beyond debate? It is a question worth pondering today because of a historic confluence of circumstances: an impending wave of charitable giving at an unprecedented level; long-term projections of federal deficits, undermining the assumption that social programs can best be funded by government; and a new generation of so-called social entrepreneurs, looking to try creative approaches to help those in need, and to do so on a large scale. These circumstances, moreover, emerge in the context of heightened, post-[Hurricane] Katrina public dissatisfaction with the quality of government-provided public services. Together, they suggest the possibility of imagining a modern society where major social service efforts are provided on a large scale outside the government, through privately funded, not-for-profit charitable organizations.

Reform Mismanagement

In the era before passage of the Social Security Act in 1935, whose Title V provided for such spending, privately funded agencies yielded the bulk of U.S. social services, augmented by such local public institutions as poorhouses, asylums and orphanages. Nevertheless, such agencies—and groups like the Child Welfare League of America—assumed that government services would be at least as good as their private, often religiously inspired predecessors, as well as more universal in reach and standardized in approach, and thus preferable. They did not oppose government social service spending, and, indeed, were often among its leading advocates.

In any event, greater government social service spending was certainly achieved. In terms of quality, however, it is hard to argue that things have worked out the way reformers intended. Consider services for children. [Since 1996], 22 to 36 children have died each year under the watch of New York City's Administration for Children and Families. A recent federal review of state child welfare agencies found that not a single state complied fully with federal standards. Then there's Head Start, whose potent name, and the fact that it provides grants to local organizations in every state, has made it immune to budget cuts. Yet a 2005 federal study involving 383 sites and 4,600 children found it led to no gains in math learning, oral comprehension or motivation to learn.

Increasing Private Philanthropy

This record of government-provided services plays out today in a dramatically changing environment for philanthropy. In recognition of the wealth of soon-to-retire boomers, the Boston College Center on Wealth and Philanthropy estimates that

Keeping Government Out of Charity Work

It is important to realize that shifting from government-run welfare to private charity does not mean that government should fund those charities.

President, [George W.] Bush has proposed that faith-based charities be eligible to receive billions of dollars in federal grants to provide social services. But, in doing so, he risks mixing government and charity in a way that could undermine the very things that have made private charity so effective.

Government dollars come with strings attached and raise serious questions regarding the separation of church and state. Charities that accept government funds could find themselves overwhelmed with paperwork and subject to a host of federal regulations. The potential for government meddling is tremendous, and even if the regulation is not abused, it will require a redirection of scarce resources away from charitable activities and toward administrative functions. Officials of charities may end up spending more time reading the *Federal Register* than the Bible.

Cato Handbook on Policy, *6th edition, 2005.*

philanthropic giving will total some $6 trillion between 2003 and 2050. Already, [since 1996], there's been an 88% increase in the number of foundations. Over the [same period] there has been a 67% growth in the overall number of U.S. non-profits.

Meanwhile, a wave of capable persons has come forward to establish effective new social service organizations, based on new ideas and with little or no government support. Indeed, it can be argued that we are now in an unprecedented period for the emergence of such people, who have started new types of job training, mentoring and immigrant-assistance efforts. The term "social entrepreneur"—for those who establish such organizations—has entered the language and become current on college campuses, where courses and research centers (Harvard, Duke, Stanford) on the topic have been established.

Thus the stars are aligned for nongovernmental organizations to play a much larger role in assisting those in need. To date, however, the [George W.] Bush administration, in part as a matter of political pragmatism, has seen such groups less as substitutes for the welfare state than as potential new beneficiaries of it—directing federal resources toward faith-based groups formerly independent of government, in an effort to "level the playing field" with nonreligious contractors. A case can be made, however, that a truly independent, philanthropically supported nonprofit sector can better sidestep the pitfalls that have plagued government. Such a sector would be likely to attract committed employees and volunteers. This was certainly the case pre-New Deal. More to the point, the willingness of Americans to answer a call to service continues to be strong, as reflected by the emergence of major new "brand name" nonprofits such as Teach for America, Prison Fellowship and Habitat for Humanity.

Private Organizations Better Suited

What's more, service organizations which rely on private donations—whether from individuals or foundations—might actually prove to be more accountable for their performance than their public or publicly funded counterparts. It is hard to imagine a private organization surviving the bad publicity and subsequent fall-off in donations which might follow the death of children in its care. Indeed, the possibility of organizations being punished for poor performance was demonstrated by the sharp drop in donations to the national United Way organization following corruption charges involving its executive director. In contrast, public employee unions, influential with legislatures, make it more difficult to discipline public social service agencies similarly.

The transition to a diminished government role in social services would be complex, as Americans have been conditioned for several generations to view government as the provider of first resort. And the substitute for government could not be small, volunteer-based organizations, 19th-century style—although small, voluntary groups will, and should, always be with us. Rather, large-scale, professionally staffed brand name agencies of proven effectiveness would be needed—much as brand name chains of charter schools are now emerging. This would require the development of sophisticated tools to match the coming wave of philanthropy with the places where it will do the most good.

Such tools might include a stock market equivalent for major service-providing nonprofits. This is not as odd as it sounds; serious people are already considering such an idea. They include George Overholser—a founding member of the financial services firm, Capital One, now with the National Nonprofit Finance Fund—who argues that a means must be developed so that donors can distinguish between "build" capital and "buy" capital. The former would support new, unproven ideas, the latter the expansion of proven successes. Mr. Overholser envisions a quasi-stock market in which "venture philanthropists" might put their funds at risk to support a social entrepreneur's new idea. If the idea can be implemented effectively, a second wave of donors would repay the original venture philanthropists with interest, allowing the latter to have their capital back and be free to move on to new nonprofit startups. A philanthropic "market" of this kind would, naturally, require the equivalent of rating agencies.

Such a system would, to be sure, have to emerge gradually—after all, the general replacement of private with public sector social services did not occur overnight. But the question of whether and how to do so should be part of any discussion about the present and future of the welfare state.

Periodical Bibliography

The following articles have been selected to supplement the diverse views presented in this chapter.

Adam Cohen	"When Wall Street Runs Welfare," *Time*, March 23, 1998.
Ronald Cohen	"Helping the Poor Become Rich," *Global Agenda*, January 2006.
Economist	"The Compassionate Capitalist," August 6, 2005.
Corine Hegland	"What Works for Welfare?" *National Journal*, January 10, 2004.
Edward Iwata	"Businesses Grow More Socially Conscious," *USA Today*, February 14, 2007.
Dafna Izenberg	"We Pay Cash for Good Behaviour," *Maclean's*, December 17, 2007.
Susan E. McGregor	"Welfare Isn't Working," *Amsterdam* (NY) *News*, December 1, 2005.
New Republic	"Fared Well," September 4, 2006.
Joyce Purnick	"Freedom Rings, but the Bills Don't Get Paid," *New York Times*, January 24, 2005.
Pearl Wang	"Investing with a Good Conscience," *Business Week*, April 24, 2004.
David Wessel	"In Poverty Tactics, an Old Debate: Who Is at Fault?" *Wall Street Journal*, June 15, 2006.

For Further Discussion

Chapter 1

1. In discussing the impact of welfare reform, Ron Haskins and Cecilio Morales refer to the government's welfare-to-work agenda. What kind of evidence does Haskins use to argue that this agenda has been successful? What evidence does Morales use to suggest that the strategy has been a failure? Whose arguments do you find more convincing? Explain why.

2. Douglas J. Besharov argues that welfare reform should not be considered a complete success. Explain why this author believes welfare reform has not gone far enough; then declare whether you agree with any of his assessments. If you do agree with some or all of his claims, clarify your reasoning. If you do not find any of his arguments compelling, explain why you disagree with them.

3. After reading all the viewpoints in this chapter, explain what, if any, elements of the 1996 welfare reform laws you consider advantageous to the poor and the nation as a whole. Then, explain what shortcomings the law may have, in your opinion. Support your claims with examples from the viewpoints.

Chapter 2

1. Robert E. Rector and Melissa G. Pardue assert that the erosion of marriage is responsible for many current social problems and that the marriage-related goals of the 1996 welfare reform legislation should be reinforced with stronger policies. Sharon Lerner maintains that government promotion of marriage is an ineffective strategy that is limited to a narrow approach to the institution of mar-

riage. Which viewpoint makes the more convincing argument in your opinion? Why?

2. Josefina Figueira-McDonough makes the point that government administrators are neglecting a political problem: the need for welfare recipients who are required to work outside their homes to provide care for their children. Christine Carter McLaughlin and Kristin Luker fault government policy makers for presenting "teenage pregnancy"—or, more exactly, pregnancies among unmarried women—as a political problem. Which problem do you think is more serious? Support your position with examples from the viewpoints and any personal experiences.

3. The national debate about the effectiveness of the current welfare system and the future of welfare policies has gotten off track, Nancy K. Cauthen argues. According to Cauthen, the needs of children should be returned to the center of this debate. What do you think is at the center of the debate right now? Explain, citing examples from this or other viewpoints.

Chapter 3

1. Rachel Alexander contends that illegal immigrants are a drain on public services and that the government could stem illegal immigration by cutting off access to these services. Douglas S. Massey, on the other hand, argues that most illegal immigrants do not use public services because they fear having contact with government agencies. After reading these viewpoints, do you think illegal immigrants are a burden on the welfare state? In framing your answer, be sure to use quotes from both viewpoints—indicating why you agree with some of the quoted claims and why you disagree with the opposing views.

2. According to Rich Lowry, how does the food stamp program have "all the worst features of the old pre-reform welfare"? Do you agree with Lowry's assessment? Ex-

plain why or why not. What reasons does Linda Bopp provide to support her claim that food stamp allowances should not be cut? Do Bopp's arguments undermine Lowry's assertions? Why or why not?

3. All of the authors in this chapter discuss the impact of welfare upon children. Referring to food stamps, immigration, noncustodial fathers, and any other aspect of the welfare system, explain whether you believe welfare programs are teaching dependence to future generations.

Chapter 4

1. Michael Sherraden is a well-known advocate of individual development accounts (IDAs) and their ability to provide poor people with gainful employment as well as assets. As he contends, such small-scale efforts have been utilized in some areas to build the assets of those who take advantage of these accounts. He acknowledges, though, that these projects may not be able to reach everyone in need at the same time. That is, in some circumstances "it may be necessary to start small but with a policy design that can be expanded over time." Jared Bernstein agrees that IDAs are often too small to have an immediate effect on universal welfare policy; however, he goes on to claim that because these projects are too insignificant, they should be ignored in addressing poverty because they distract from finding more large-scale solutions. Do you believe that asset-building strategies are a worthwhile strategy that should be expanded, or do you think that Bernstein's assessment is more valid? Explain using the arguments from these viewpoints.

2. What arguments do Joyce A. Klein, Ilgar Alisultanov, and Amy Kays Blair use to support their view that microenterprise can help some low-income individuals secure assets and earn a supplementary income, if not a sole income? What arguments does Nancy Jurik employ to counter the

benefits of self-employment solutions? Whose viewpoint do you think is more convincing? Explain why.

3. Charles Murray maintains that giving all Americans a tax-funded monetary account that could be tapped for any purpose would make people more financially and socially responsible. Dalton Conley, however, believes that handing out block grants and taking welfare away from the government will not create a social utopia because modern life demands more of people's time than their money. Do you think that stripping government of welfare duties and making communities responsible for their own welfare will unite Americans in the way Murray suggests? Why or why not? In answering the question, be sure to clarify whether you think one of the functions of government is to ensure the welfare of the poor and disadvantaged.

Organizations to Contact

The editors have compiled the following list of organizations concerned with the issues debated in this book. The descriptions are derived from materials provided by the organizations. All have publications or information available for interested readers. The list was compiled on the date of publication of the present volume; the information provided here may change. Be aware that many organizations take several weeks or longer to respond to inquiries, so allow as much time as possible.

Bread for the World
50 F St. NW, Suite 500, Washington, DC 20001
(202) 639-9400 • fax: (202) 639-9401
e-mail: bread@bread.org
Web site: www.bread.org

Bread for the World is a Christian organization attempting to end hunger worldwide by lobbying the U.S. government to institute policies that support this goal. The group conducts research and creates educational projects to find ways to fight hunger and address associated problems such as poverty, education, health care, and housing. Welfare reform has been addressed directly in Bread for the World's policy statements as well as in its research papers such as *Working Harder for Working Families: Hunger 2008*, the organization's most recent report on the state of world hunger.

Cato Institute
1000 Massachusetts Ave. NW, Washington, DC 20001
(202) 842-0200 • fax: (202) 842-3490
Web site: www.cato.org

The Cato Institute, a libertarian, public policy research organization, advocates for limited government and complete observation of the principles of democracy in all government institutions. Accordingly, Cato applauds the positive effects of the welfare reform instituted under the Clinton administration, which reduced the amount of government financial assistance given in welfare programs. The organization continues to promote the ability of private charities to aid the poor as opposed to government intervention and aid. Publications of the institute include the tri-annual *Cato Journal* and the quarterly *Cato's Letter*. Policy analysis reports as well as individual commentary by institute scholars discuss the issues of welfare in the United States.

Economic Policy Institute (EPI)
1333 H St. NW, Suite 300, East Tower
Washington, DC   20005
(202) 775-8810 • fax: (202) 775-0819
e-mail: epi@epi.org
Web site: www.epi.org

EPI promotes policies within the government that provide equal opportunities for all individuals working within the American economy. Specifically, the institute advocates for the interests of workers whose incomes fall in the low to middle range, providing these people with a voice in the national economic policy debate. When studying economic policy, the organization analyzes the impact of government decisions on the living standards of the working class. Welfare reform has been the topic of articles in the tri-annual *EPI Journal* as well as in other policy analysis and commentary papers, available on the organization's Web site.

Foundation for Economic Education (FEE)
30 S. Broadway, Irvington-on-Hudson, NY   10533
toll-free: (800) 960-4FEE
e-mail: comments@fee.org
Web site: www.fee.org

Founded in 1946, FEE works to provide a counterweight to what it sees as the alarming disregard for the fundamental ideals on which the American government was founded. These fundamental principles include the importance of private property, liberty, rule of law, free-market economic policies, and freedom of choice. FEE offers numerous educational resources and programs on topics associated with the principles of the "freedom philosophy," as well as the periodic publications the *Freeman: Ideas on Liberty* and *Notes from FEE*. On the issue of welfare reform, the foundation argues that government-funded aid will not reduce poverty in the long run and in fact produces harmful consequences such as dependence and increased government spending.

The Heritage Foundation
214 Massachusetts Ave. NE, Washington, DC   20002
(202) 546-4400 • fax: (202) 546-8328
e-mail: info@heritage.org
Web site: www.heritage.org

The Heritage Foundation is a conservative public policy research institute dedicated to the promotion of liberty, a free-market economy, and a strong national defense. Reduction of both welfare payments and the number of individuals dependent entirely on welfare aid are two key principles of the welfare reform policies supported by the foundation. Papers by the institute analyzing issues related to welfare reform include "The Continuing Good News About Welfare Reform," "Understanding Poverty in America," and "Welfare Reform and the Healthy Marriage Initiative."

National Center for Law and Economic Justice (NCLEJ)
275 Seventh Ave., Suite 1506, New York, NY   10001-6708
(212) 633-6967
e-mail: info@nclej.org
Web site: www.nclej.org

Since its founding in 1965, NCLEJ has worked to ensure, through legal measures, that low-income individuals have been afforded all the rights and opportunities they are guaranteed by the Constitution. Through litigation, policy research, and advocacy for low-income families, the center aids families and individuals in need. Through its reports and advocacy efforts, NCLEJ tackles issues relating to poverty, such as food stamps, health care, and employment. Issue-specific reports, in addition to periodic reports on the state of poverty in the United States, are available on the organization's Web site.

National Organization for Women (NOW)
1100 H St. NW, 3rd Fl., Washington, DC   20005
(202) 628-8669 • fax: (202) 785-8576
Web site: www.now.org

Dedicated to helping women achieve equal and full participation in society, the feminist advocacy group NOW works to educate the public about discrimination in American society and to provide opportunities for individuals to become involved in policy-changing activities such as voting, protesting, and letter writing. The organization sees welfare reform and poverty reduction as important issues related to larger problems in American society such as violence against women, sex discrimination, and racism. Articles published by the organization, such as "Poverty Reduction Must Include Reproductive Health Options" and "Poverty Right Here at Home Increases for Second Year in a Row," tackle the issues of welfare reform and the shortcomings in poverty-reduction policies in the United States.

Poverty and Race Research Action Council (PRRAC)
1015 Fifteenth St. NW, Suite 400, Washington, DC   20005
(202) 906-8023 • fax: (202) 842-2885
e-mail: info@prrac.org
Web site: www.prrac.org

PRRAC, a civil rights policy organization, sponsors research efforts to explore the connections between poverty and race and provides educational outreach in the forms of the bimonthly publication *Poverty & Race* and the civil rights history curriculum guide *Putting the Movement Back into Civil Rights Teaching*. The council uses this information to advocate for government policy that provides greater equality within

American society. Numerous articles outlining the state of welfare in America are available on the organization's Web site under the topic "Poverty/Welfare."

Progressive Policy Institute (PPI)
600 Pennsylvania Ave. SE, Suite 400, Washington, DC   20003
(202) 547-0001 • fax: (202) 544-5014
Web site: www.ppionline.org

PPI offers a third alternative to the current conservative and liberal debate within the U.S. political system, promoting government policies that are progressive in addressing the new challenges of the Information Age and that are created to serve the people. With regard to welfare, the institute advocates for policies that empower those living in poverty in the United States to achieve independence and not remain recipients of government aid that confines them to lives of poverty. Policy reports such as "Making Work Pay" directly address the problems with welfare in the United States and strategies for combating the current situation.

Urban Institute
2100 M St. NW, Washington, DC   20037
(202) 833-7200
Web site: www.urban.org

The Urban Institute works to ensure that implementation of public policy benefits people at all economic and social levels living within the urban environments of the United States and abroad. The institute encourages public debate about issues such as crime, education, housing, and welfare and researches and promotes policies that appropriately address these topics. Reports discussing the impact of welfare reform, such as "Getting On, Staying On, and Getting Off Welfare: The Complexity of State-by-State Policy Choices," "Is There a System Supporting Low-Income Families?" and "The Effect of Specific Welfare Policies on Poverty," are available on the organization's Web site.

Bibliography of Books

Rebecca M. Blank, Sheldon H. Danziger, and Rober F. Schoeni, eds.
Working and Poor: How Economic and Policy Changes Are Affecting Low-Wage Workers. New York: Russell Sage Foundation, 2002.

Robert D. Cherry
Welfare Transformed: Universalizing Family Policies That Work. New York: Oxford University Press, 2007.

Jason DeParle
American Dream: Three Women, Ten Kids, and a Nation's Drive to End Welfare. New York: Penguin, 2005.

Greg J. Duncan, Aletha C. Huston, and Thomas S. Weisner
Higher Ground: New Hope for the Working Poor and Their Children. New York: Russell Sage Foundation, 2007.

Martin Gilens
Why Americans Hate Welfare: Race, Media, and the Politics of Antipoverty Policy. Chicago: University of Chicago Press, 1999.

Jeffrey Grogger and Lynn A. Karoly
Welfare Reform: Effects of a Decade of Change. Santa Monica, CA: RAND Corporation, 2005.

Jacob S. Hacker
The Divided Welfare State: The Battle over Public and Private Social Benefits in the United States. New York: Cambridge University Press, 2002.

Joel F. Handler and Yeheskel Hasenfeld
Blame Welfare, Ignore Poverty and Inequality. New York: Cambridge University Press, 2007.

Ron Haskins   *Work over Welfare: The Inside Story of the 1996 Welfare Reform Law.* Washington, DC: Brookings Institution, 2006.

Sharon Hays   *Flat Broke with Children: Women in the Age of Welfare Reform.* New York: Oxford University Press, 2003.

Christopher Howard   *The Welfare State Nobody Knows: Debunking Myths About U.S. Social Policy.* Princeton, NJ: Princeton University Press, 2007.

Nancy C. Jurik   *Bootstrap Dreams: U.S. Microenterprise Development in an Era of Welfare Reform.* Ithaca, NY: ILR Press, 2005.

Kevin Lang   *Poverty and Discrimination.* Princeton, NJ: Princeton University Press, 2007.

Adrian Nicole LeBlanc   *Random Family: Love, Drugs, Trouble, and Coming of Age in the Bronx.* New York: Scribner, 2003.

Charles Murray   *In Our Hands: A Plan to Replace the Welfare State.* Washington, DC: AEI Press, 2006.

Benjamin I. Page and James R. Simmons   *What Government Can Do: Dealing with Poverty and Inequality.* Chicago: University of Chicago Press, 2000.

Christopher Pierson   *Beyond the Welfare State? The New Political Economy of Welfare.* University Park: Pennsylvania State University Press, 2007.

Jill Quadagno — *The Color of Welfare: How Racism Undermined the War on Poverty.* New York: Oxford University Press, 1995.

Jennifer A. Reich — *Fixing Families: Parents, Power, and the Child Welfare System.* New York: Routledge, 2005.

Harrell R. Rodgers — *American Poverty in a New Era of Reform.* Armonk, NY: M.E. Sharpe, 2006.

Daniel Shapiro — *Is the Welfare State Justified?* New York: Cambridge University Press, 2007.

Kathleen M. Shaw, et al. — *Putting Poor People to Work: How the Work-First Idea Eroded College Access for the Poor.* New York: Russell Sage Foundation, 2006.

David K. Shipler — *The Working Poor: Invisible in America.* New York: Knopf, 2004.

Joan Shireman — *Critical Issues in Child Welfare,* New York: Columbia University Press, 2003.

Brian Steensland — *The Failed Welfare Revolution: America's Struggle over Guaranteed Income Policy.* Princeton, NJ: Princeton University Press, 2007.

Robert Phillip Stoker and Laura Ann Wilson — *When Work Is Not Enough: State and Federal Policies to Support Needy Workers.* Washington, DC: Brookings Institution, 2006.

Index